FABULA RUSTICI

FABULA RUSTICI

or

THE BUMPKIN PLAY

A METAPHYSICAL DIALOGUE ON TRUTH AND BEING

Edited by C.J.C. Pickstock

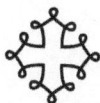

Angelico Press

First published in the USA
by Angelico Press 2025
Copyright © C.J.C. Pickstock 2025

For information, address:
Angelico Press, Ltd.
169 Monitor St.
Brooklyn, NY 11222
www.angelicopress.com

Ppr 979-8-89280-098-3
Cloth 979-8-89280-099-0

Cover design by Annabel Lee
Book design by Michael Schrauzer

For my moste chered frend,
B. A. C. Windeatt PhD, LittD

CONTENTS

EDITOR'S PREFACE

FOR MANY YEARS, THE SHORT AND UNEDITED dialogue, *Fabula Rustici*, included in an eighteenth-century *omnegadrium*, or miscellany of religious dramas, now known as Crozier FR M. a. 172, was assumed to be an anomalous metaphysical drama that did not belong to any mystery cycles or textual traditions. As is well known, *Fabula Rustici* has been the subject of many studies, analysing its atypical features, tracing evidence of provenance and "textual interferences," and so forth. However, the present edition throws new light on that apparently isolated text. Following a serendipitous discovery, it appears that *Fabula Rustici* is a shorter version of a much longer and probably more ancient play known as *The Bumpkin Play*, or *Bumpkeen Plaiye*, which appears to have a complex set of variants, traditions and tributaries. The present edition will open up that complex textual transmission by presenting the most compendious extant version of the play for modern readers, whilst noting departures from other extant and newly unearthed versions.

THE PROVENANCE OF THE BUMPKIN PLAY AND ITS TEXTUAL TRADITIONS

Almost nothing is known about the origin, authorship or tradition of the present text. Although many generations of Cambridge – and now more widely dispersed – students of Philosophical Theology, English, Islamic Philosophy, Jewish Philosophy, Comparative Literature and Modern and Medieval Languages have taken part in *ad hoc* performances and readings of the play, little is known about how or when it came to be in circulation.

The present Editor has pieced together what she can of the play's manuscript and textual transmission and tradition(s). In 1995, when the Editor had been appointed to her first academic position as a Research Fellow at Emmanuel College, Cambridge, she was invited by the late Brian Hebblethwaite to present a lecture to the Philosophy of Religion MPhil cohort on Saint Thomas

Aquinas' *Quaestiones Disputatae de Veritate*, Questions 1 to 4, in a
room high up on All Saints Passage, an annex of the old Divinity
School. It was to be her first experience of graduate teaching,
and she was understandably daunted. As luck would have it,
she had inherited rooms in Emmanuel previously occupied by
an unnamed Fellow who had since resigned from the College,
leaving behind several foolscap box-files and miscellaneous items
of debris, including some animal costumes (specifically, several
tails of different kinds and lengths, and pairs of furry ears and
paw-mittens, badly assailed by the moth). One of the boxes was
intriguingly labelled, in inky miniscule, "Aq. *De Ver.*" It contained
loose pages of a manually typed document, *The Bumpkin Plaiye*,
folded inside a large plain piece of blotting paper on which a long-
ago ink pen had tried out its fluency, leaving feathery flourishes
which had first spread themselves out, and later retreated to palest
blue. [1] Beneath the typed title was a subtitle, or an alternative title
perhaps, written by hand, larger-faced this time, reading *Fabula
Rustici* (Feast of All Souls), and then, in parenthesis, the following
plea: *(Pray for my soul!)*.

The first bundle that the Editor lifted out of the box was short
compared with the present edition, as it turns out, and ended at
the moment when God exits the stage "*equitando*," having adjudi-
cated in the discussion between S. Thomas and Mr No-Nonsense.

Beneath that enveloped sheaf lay an apparently older text on
now yellowing paper, bound by fading pink ties, written entirely
by hand, the pages being in places quite badly food-stained, and
with ink blotches sometimes obscuring whole words. This second
version also ended at the point of the divine *exitus*. [2] And beneath
that version, in the same box, were several loose fragments, some
folded slightly in the middle, unbound, apparently written entirely
in Middle English, some with folio markings and some not. Despite
the fragments' wretched state, the Editor recognised several passages
from the first encounter in Act One Scene 2 between S. Thomas
and Goobet, and several other interludes in the play.[3] All of the
pages were undated, but the Folio markings have been transferred
to the corresponding places of the text which follows.

The Editor did not realise at the time of her discovery the marvellous serendipity that the play was in fact based (loosely) upon the opening four questions of Aquinas *De Veritate*; otherwise, she might not so quickly have set this treasure aside in order to focus on the writing of her lecture. The latter passed unremarkably, but for the fact that the students, denizens of the 1980s, versed in Descartes and Kant, complained bitterly that *De Veritate* was a dreadfully difficult text full of alien concepts and frameworks which seemingly celebrated some kind of knowing beyond the limits of thought.

It was not long before the Editor returned to the Box of Plays, wondering whether it held the key to unlocking the difficult notions of S. Thomas Aquinas for her students. She consulted certain College officers who advised her to look in the College stores, and a paperchase ensued. She had identified three other versions by which she hoped (vainly, as it turned out) to complete a chronological array of variants, stemmatised for the benefit of future generations. But soon, a further version of the play appeared in her pigeon-hole (the porters having no recollection of its having been brought in),[4] yet another was handed to her in a public garden,[5] and another was discovered during a pest control operation (see below),[6] all of which raised in her the sense of a stemma that was spinning beyond her control. The Editor was given to understand that there were still earlier versions predating the founding of the College in 1584, when the site had been the seat of the Dominican Order in Cambridge. If, as some have speculated,[7] S. Thomas Aquinas visited English universities, it is not impossible that the play may have been occasioned by a visit to the Cambridge Dominican House soon after its foundation in 1238. A very complex version was apparently found by a bedmaker in an old trunk room in S. Catharine's College (as it happens, the Editor's *alma mater*) which told a story of an earlier elaborateness and intensity, later softened for a more delicate generation of readers or performers, perhaps of a pre-war golden age. Indeed, internal textual references in several versions attest to a possible early connection with, or even origination in, Katharine Hall, as it was then named, founded in

1473. Some versions mention S. Catharine in passing, though the frequent references to tears or sorrowing suggest a reference to the lachrymose S. Catharine of Siena, and not to S. Catharine of Alexandria, the philosophical Saint after whom the College was named. Another copy turned up in Highbury, North London (not too far by train from Cambridge). [8] This version included the three persons of the Trinity as distinct characters, suggesting a divergent and somewhat heretical textual tradition. And so it went on.

The Editor was later able to posit three known textual traditions, with the Cambridge lineage being the fontal source and by far the richest in terms of language, characterization, embellishment, and experimental nature. The other two traditions — emerging from Highbury and the Inner Hebridean island of Islay, respectively — appeared derivative of the Cambridge tradition, in terms of both dramatic complexity and diction. The Editor sought vainly to establish an ur-text, but in truth the many versions of the play told a story of lived performance and dilation, and not of stable textual lineages, on which more detail is given below.

There are some eight known extant manuscripts of *The Bumpkin Play*, or *Fabula Rustici*, now collected and stored in Emmanuel College, Cambridge (Emm. Coll., Cambridge, C. P. Mn. I. 17-23, c. 46r.), and several suspected manuscripts which have so far not been traced. The so-called "Floorboard MS" was found by chance in the Museum of College Life, under a loose floorboard pulled up in the late 1990s when the Maintenance Department of the College was investigating reports of scratching noises near the site of an underground conduit, a chalk stream running beneath the College. Although a majority of manuscripts were found in Cambridge over the years, several have been identified in other parts of the world, as far flung as Princeton, Bogotá and Chiang Mai, [9] and remain in private ownership in those places. The Editor is grateful for the opportunity to have consulted several (though not all) of these.

Each known manuscript that the Editor has had the privilege to examine is embellished by hand: there is no stable version of any manuscript or copy of the play. Even where there are multiple typed or printed copies of one version, apparently used by a specific group of players, each one will tend to have its own modifications: some show marginal comments such as exclamation marks or suggested translations, or less than generous asides about one player or another (e.g. "is he salutary?"), whilst others have deletions or digressions, cartoons and doodles, as well as random comments, such as "the tea is nice" or "what is that scratching noise?"

The deletions, insertions and revisions suggest circulation, repeated performance and elaboration by different theatrical groups over a duration of many years, though any attempt at a chronology of much earlier versions is now deemed impossible owing, first, to the multitude of versions and the textual focus on performance: indeed, marginalia [e.g. Crozier D. a l. 1554, "DEUS may a vumman bee, *si placet*"] suggest that original scribes and theatrical parties welcomed variations and experimentation on the occasions of its performance.[10] But a chronology of earlier versions is also, secondly, rendered impracticable by the "Terryble Fludde" of 1782 which is thought to have destroyed some archives in Katharine Hall, the establishment being quite close to the then tidal Granta river. The doomed documents may have been housed in the cellars of Sherlock Hall (demolished in 1962), carrying away on its tide a host of possible or dreamed-of stemmata.

Such obfuscations of chronological reconstruction might understandably confound any editor, but the present Editor has now reconciled herself to variousness, attributing it to the carnival mode of the play's transmission and tradition. This embrace is seen as a form of intensified sensitivity, fidelity, even, to the spirit of the play.

Another problem over which an editorial decision had to be made is the variability of spelling and the admixture of Middle English and Modern English, and, in one or two cases, Old English, as well as occasional Latin and French phrases. The rendering of key nomenclature as well as miscellaneous words is by no means standardized in any of the available manuscripts, sometimes even across the span of adjacent lines. The Editor has retained this variety where the sense remains accessible, and has indicated, and sometimes hazarded, brief interlinear translations where the sense is hard to discover for the late modern reader.

The present edition takes an inclusive approach as its editorial policy, construing the most elaborated and, as it happens, the most recently discovered version as the best example of the source tradition [C. P. Mn. I. 22 c. 46r.], known for obvious reasons as the Floorboard Edition. This text was chosen on the basis that it may have accrued the maximum number and kinds of modifications and additions, and so best represents the summation of the performance tradition of the play reckonable without too much editorial intrusion. Where there are features in other manuscripts that the Editor regards as theologically or otherwise significant or striking, she has added these with a fair degree of editorial abandon to the present edition. The editorial principle thus brazenly leans more towards compendiousness than purism, placing the event of its performance ahead of evocations of such mirages as "an original version." The Editor justifies this strategy on the basis of the many versions' own intrinsic multiplicity, and on the textual evidence, in the form of marginalia, of a focus upon the event, and away from the manuscripts as isolated or static edifices. The Editor has however been mindful to indicate her addition of such carefree inclusions in the present text in corresponding footnotes for those readers whose temperament or purposes are otherwise. Such a reader may also wish to consult Ezra Clydebounde, *The Crozier Manuscript*, for an attempt to reconstruct a possible second textual variant (c. 1977?), tracing its origin to an hotel of unknown name on Sidmouth Esplanade, South Devon.[11]

The play is a living tradition which continues to evolve. It is hoped that the publication of the present edition will encourage readers and performers to embellish and develop it still further, and by no means to treat the moment of this publication as the play's foreclosure. It is meanwhile likely that there are other versions yet to be discovered, and maybe even undiscovered traditions. The Editor notes that she has convened at least thirty readings of different versions of the play over the years that she has been a Fellow of Emmanuel College, and estimates that some four hundred and fifty students must by now possess photocopies of these, and may indeed have performed the play subsequently in their own various places, perhaps with their own embellishments and adaptations to polemical or other circumstances. During the Covid-19 Lockdown of 2020, on All Souls' Day, an online performance took place with over one hundred participants from around the world. No record was kept as to their precise number or their names.

THE PLAY'S DEDICATION

The present play is associated with a liturgical occasion, All Souls' Day. This ascription, rather like Trinity Sunday and the Feast Day of Corpus Christi, is not directly related to specific events in the life of Christ (see below). For further detail on the significance of liturgical dedications, see V. A. Kolve, ed., *The Play Called Corpus Christi*.[12]

It is not known whether this play is part of a cycle comparable to the well-known cyclic plays of Towneley, York or Chester, although there are traces of intertextual interference with or from the cyclical plays, not least the naming of its eponymous hero, Goobet, who appears briefly in the Chester Cycle. Assuming the play's provenance, as indicated at line 1, this play may be non-cyclic; or it may be the only extant portion of a cycle associated with Impyngton, recorded in the Domesday Book as Epintone; also known as Empinton, Ympiton and Impynton, meaning "place belonging to the imps," now known as Impington, Cambridgeshire. Or it may have been a "souling" play, a routine part of the activities on the Eve of All Souls, although these tended to involve death- and resurrection-themed plays, and to be presided over by Beelzebub, which is not the case with the present play.

THE THEME OF THE BUMPKIN PLAY

The *Bumpkin Playe*, or *Fabula Rustici*, is certainly atypical in taking a "scholasticall" theme, though it is by no means un-Biblical or non-Eucharistic in import (see lines 4345–50). But there are some equivalent examples, such as John Rastell, *The Four Elements* (1518), "declarynge many proper poyntys of philosophy naturall" (see lines

136-37), and Henry Medwall's interlude, *Fulgens*, probably first performed in Lambeth Palace in 1497, based on the Latin treatise *De Vera Nobilitate* by the Italian humanist Buonaccorso da Montemagno of Pistoia; and *The World and the Child* (earliest surviving edition, 1522) based on the late-fourteenth or fifteenth century poem, "The Mirror of the Periods of Man's Life."

The custom of praying for the souls of the deceased dates back to 2 *Maccabees* 12:42-46. The setting apart of a special day for intercession for certain of the faithful on 2 November was first established by S. Odilo of Cluny (d. 1048) at his Abbey in 998. From Cluny, the custom spread to the other Houses of the Cluniac order, which became the largest and most extensive network of monasteries in Europe, with Castle Acre Priory (founded in 1089) and Thetford Priory (founded in 1103), both in Norfolk, and Wangford Priory in Suffolk (founded before 1159) being the closest to Cambridge. The celebration of the souls of the faithful was adopted in several dioceses in France and spread throughout the Western Church. It was accepted in Rome in the fourteenth century. [13] There are various traditions of dramatic productions taking place on the Eve of All Souls, known as "souling plays," as mentioned above, together with associated practices, some of which appear to be referred to in the present play, such as the use of turnips to make ghoulish lanterns, and the eating of "soul cakes" (see lines 1312, and 3564 and 2582, respectively).

The Feast of All Souls certainly provides rich *topoi* for Guild players (perhaps in this case the Guild of Gravediggers, though this is pure speculation on the Editor's part, and is not mentioned in any available version), from death and mourning, the metaphysics of the soul, the nature of God, divine visitation, redemption, and, in the case of this rather philosophical play, the nature of truth. The saintly and "souling" season, when the veil between the living and the dead is at its most permeable, may account for the simultaneous appearance of otherwise historically disparate characters, walking together about the Grene, as if time and eternity had bumped into one another and gone for a stroll. The play's setting in early November may also occasion the many references to foul weather throughout the play.

A NOTE ON PLACE

The topical indication in the rubric at line 1 gives clear reference as to dramatic provenance, whether an imagined or actual setting and performance. This is confirmed by a study of the play's linguistic features, which, following the publication of *A Linguistic Atlas of Late Medieval English* (1986),[14] enables the Editor to identify traces of Cambridgeshire dialect and linguistic fields. Professor Richard Beadle's DPhil dissertation, "The Medieval Drama of East Anglia: Studies in Dialect, Documentary Records and Stagecraft" (University of York, 1977), further supports this observation. The juxtaposition of aureate and demotic diction is indicative of the mixed demography of this region, from its learned inhabitants to "unlettered" bumpkins who prefer to avoid the University area (e.g. lines 1255–58). Victor Scherb's *Staging Faith: East Anglian Drama in the Later Middle Ages*, as well as Nelson (ed.), *Records of Early English*, are instructive secondary sources on this point.[15]

"The Grene" referred to at various points throughout the play, and often used as a topographical eponym of its protagonist, Goobet-on-the-Green, is the apparently confined or unified site of the play's action. It may have been demarcated by a raised platform, or it may have referred to the Village Green itself.[16] The Green of Impington Village itself extended farther than it does today, encompassing the area now surrounding S. Andrews Church, leading to Burgoyne's Road. There are no specific directions as to stagecraft in any of the extant manuscripts regarding the erection of a raised platform, except that a scaffold is mentioned (e.g. lines 3081 and 4461 ff.). But see Meredith and Tailby, *The Staging of Religious Drama* and Sumiko Miyajima, *The Theatre of Man*, on the limitations of physical circumstance, especially in the light of the references to foul weather and wintry conditions (e.g. "thawing fot-maidens," line 19).[17]

The play may be said to have suffered from the critical neglect of East Anglian theatre more generally. See for example, Granger, *The N-Town Play*. And on likely rural, parish-based productions in East Anglia, see John Coldewey, "The non-cycle plays and the East Anglian tradition."[18] This play is at least "typical" of East Anglian dramas in not fitting into a single paradigm.[19] Despite its

metaphysical theme, the play's picaresque structure of successive
philosophical, absurd and sometimes mystical encounters, and final
liturgical *synaxis* and *afflatus*, festive dance and implied Beatific
exaltation, are not uncharacteristic of the exorbitant theatricality
of medieval English plays.[20]

WOMEN IN THE BUMPKIN PLAY

It is notable that earlier manuscripts of the play contain no women
characters, although, as mentioned in the foregoing, there are
indications that women performers took part (e.g. FR M. a. 172),
notably at times even playing exalted roles, such as DEUS. If this
was a University-related play, then one may recall that women
were not granted full membership of the University of Cambridge
until 1948, when the first degrees were awarded to women. But
there were significant philosophically minded women associated
with Cambridge at different periods, such as Margaret Cavendish,
Duchess of Newcastle-Upon-Tyne (1623-1673) and Lady Anne
Conway (1631-1679), both of whom were connected with Cambridge Platonism in the seventeenth century, and especially with
Emmanuel and Christ's Colleges. It is perhaps no surprise that
there is an interlude in some versions of the play in which Goobet
discourses loftily with Margaret and Anne, and indeed, one notes
that allusions to and invocations of their poetic and philosophic
diction are detectable in these illuminating and edified discussions
(see Act One, Scene Two). Several versions include a fleeting and
perhaps slightly comical appearance of Geoffrey Chaucer's Wife of
Bath, strewing cabbages and turnips as she runs through, cursing
the corruption and laziness of "lymytours and [...] hooly freres"
(lines 1306-7). Several later versions, in the Cambridge textual
tradition, include a scene of three women known to have been
a strength and inspiration to illuminated men: "Three Mystical
Women." These are Monica, the mother of S. Augustine, Macrina,
the elder sister of S. Gregory of Nyssa, and Diotima of Mantinaea,
whose doctrine of Eros is central to Plato's *Symposium*. The scene
culminates in the appearance of Beatrice, she of Dante's *Com-
media*, who guides Dante the character to a higher metaphysical

estate. Her mystical and somewhat Marian summation of the play appears to draw together the various local diegetic digressions with the whole universe, suggesting an ascent and fulfilment of all the characters, both living and dead, of all souls, who "through Godes grace | Are throngyng fast" (lines 45-47) into the final dance. Their numinous discussions are seemingly in asymmetrical relation with the ribald and confounding scene of the Four Drunken Tribesmen, in which there is one perhaps apocryphal line (included in the current version, though it was under ink erasure in the Floorboard MS) which expresses uncertainty as to "why | Ther ar womyn" (lines 3659-60). These later versions are certainly ripe for a feminist reading, and especially in relation to mystical theology.

THE THEOLOGY OF THE BUMPKIN PLAY

Scholarship to date has focussed on *Fabula Rustici* as epiphenomenal to other developments, such as the representation of women in medieval theatre,[21] zoomorphism as a sublimation of the loss of *analogia entis* (as it was later termed) in metaphysics,[22] and representations of holy orders in late medieval literature.[23] But little has been written on the theology of this play in its own right, except insofar as it offers an example of primitive religiosity of simple uneducated folk, and strangely, or perhaps not, much of this has come from Continental Europe. Tatyana Fitchmeyer's monumental *Gott oder Bumpkin: Was soll es sein?* (1981) corrects an imbalance by attending to the motivations of Happy Pilgrim and their covert centrality to the play as after all a Biblically based morality play,[24] while Moses Tremblay's essay, "Qui est Monsieur No-Nonsense? Au cœur de *Fabula Rustici*" (2012) in *Etudes de théâtre médiéval obscure* instructively discredits those accounts which tend to dismiss Mr No-Nonsense as an ephemeral character, or caricature.[25]

The reader may note the distinctive characterisation of DEUS as authoritative and scholarly, discoursing on the attributes of God Himself as Trinity, and adjudicating in the discussion of truth almost as if he were attending a research seminar. As in *The Castle of Perseverance*, DEUS enters late in the discussion. However, in

the present play, God's entry marks a distinctive shift in theatrical
tone, from discursive, disputational and at times stichomythic, to
mystical and apophatic, with lamentation and rejoicing, turn by
turn, leading to an overall sense of eschatological realisation and
good cheer. We see the gradually expanding circular dance pageant
into which the players variously enter, forming a roundel, echoing
the convertibility of the transcendentals whose "cercle | Or daunce
of graces" (lines 1412–13) traces the spiralling interplay between
the persons of the Trinity. Indeed, a distinctive Trinitarian theology underlies the play, of a God who is present to Himself, and
to all else, and paradoxically present as an ultimate interpersonal
mediation. In the zograscopic dance of the mystical women, the
theology of the play is condensed:

> We generate one an-other
> Through our folwable steppes;
> 4445   Our "three" is al-so
> "Ffour" and "ffive"!
>   As for the seraphim
> Who merge movement
> And sight,
> 4450   And are al-redy
>   At their goal,
> And yet contynuyingly fly,
>   There is no visioun of Love
> Without the engendering and
> 4455   Mouemente of Love,
> Al-times reciprocall,
>   Al-wey bynding to-gether,
> With wei-la and joie,
>   Unknoueinge and knoueing,
> 4460   Counterposen parfitly.
>   We chaunt, encercle and see!

For Diotima, the mystical women's singing, encircling and seeing
entail an angelic binding of all disparate things, including sorrow
with joy, knowing and unknowing – recalling Anne's "gostely
cognacioun, | Tourning bitwyx | Soliditee and aeyriyalitee" (lines

607-9). Here one may infer that the play's pattern of successive dialogues gives rise by contagion of "mutuall embraces" to a multitudinous *synaxis*, or joining-together: a third, and then a fourth, to a host of bystanders and unexpected travellers, to whom we make the promise of our own continued dance, and owe an obligation to cast our words headlong into their futurity, even though this may be attended by our own mortal vanishing. In the same way, one may infer that we as readers or spectators of the play are not the only or final intended recipients of this text; future and indeed long past people, the living and the dead, are brought within its compass, for this is the Eve of All Souls. The play is articulated by pointers and reminders of a temporal and eschatological future: the comically literal anticipations of future philosophers who will one day come to solve a particular puzzle or propose an argument (e.g. line 1206-8), and a future time "[w]hen peple | Will *lose all wondringe*" (lines 2462-64), and will be foolish enough to climb "montayns, | With raggish and daffed | Lingel and cabeling" (lines 2058-63); but also the thronging souls in Goobet's opening Banns who set the cosmic scope of the play's diegetic chronotope, and the saints to whom Christ's body is "evenly forscatered" in the Church (lines 4336-37). S. Thomas glimpses the eschatological day, "When we wyll | Bicome | The very medium | Ourselves" (lines 4366-69).

Above all, transcendent relationality between the persons of the Godhead is the condition of possibility for these earthly kinships and mediations: they are responses to, reflections of and participations in the "infenite | Dyvyne enlumining" (lines 4497-98). The Father and the Son are immediately co-present, and yet, this immediacy is the mediation of the shared "spirit" of their encounter, the span of desire, which is present from the beginning, but transmitted through their relation from moment to moment. Bringing together diverse currents of the Patristic tradition, Spirit is the product of Father and Son, as the bond of love, following Augustine, and yet is also the breath in which the Father utters the Son, following the Cappadocians.

The all-inclusive dance and *afflatus* with which the *Bumpkin Play* concludes are suggestive of a high theology of universal salvation, or *apokatastasis*: the gathering-in and restoration of all creation to the estate of perfection. The dispirited and gloom-inducing discussants whom Goobet encounters in the early scenes of the play, who variously delimit truth towards the "dong-hep" of either negativity or positivistic boundedness, seem, despite their fallen notions, to be included in Beatrice's call to "y-tourn" (line 4464) and to be exalted in the final dance (line 4499). One notes that the hostile and sceptical characters who had mocked Goobet for his rustic ("lumpen") disposition are also part of this final elevation, and, one supposes, even the drunken tribesmen of the Tribe of Naturalists (as suggested by the zoomorphism of the rubric at line 4499 ff., that the dancing be *"accompanyed by a certayn amount of braying,"* though certainly there is no donkey in that tribe, as far as we know). This redemptive final curtain flourish places a liturgical or even theurgical freight on the dramatic proceedings themselves, as witnessed most directly by Mr No-Nonsense's change of heart (around line 4075). Though indeed it takes the drastic circumstance of God's physical descent and conversation with him to effect this otherwise cheering *volte-face*.

The exchange between Goobet and Aquinas concerning the incarnation, or "walkynge-trewth" (lines 4293 ff.), and its eucharistic savour (lines 4345–50), situate the conversation in a Trinitarian context. Indeed, DEUS refers to himself directly in Trinitarian terms, as "the thrilli-hod" (line 3982), determined several times in terms of circular movement or dance, reminding the spectators of the transcendentals being described in similar terms earlier in the discussion (e.g., lines 1376 ff., 1565–67, 4394). The numinous discussion between Goobet, Margaret and Anne takes the Trinitarian context as all-encompassing: "Therr are only | Thre Realitiees: | Godd, | Chryst, & Spirit" (lines 624–26), with all of creaturely life turning upon Christ, the "Holy Pivott" (line 628).

Goobet's closing *paean* indicates that it may have been mistaken to think of truth as a thing or datum to be observed or debated, or else as an endlessly postponed hollowed-out nullity, utterly without delight or glory. Rather, truth is the arrival of a lived relation between goodness, truth and beauty, leading to an "accord" or alignment between God and humanity. One surmises that at the

conclusion of the play, the spectators themselves may also join in
the dance (especially if the beer was indeed provided by the Boot
Inn, or Public House), [26] performing the uplifting message of the
play, and, as it were, dancing themselves into the communion of
saints. This accord is itself the path to bliss: the soul already tarries
in Paradise with the blessed (lines 4505 ff.).

But what of those disappointing conversations with the self-
vaunting "[d]reary felowys" (line 1627) whom Goobet interrogates in
the earlier scenes of the play? And what of ourselves, the separated
and extrinsic spectators or readers, all in our own spheres? Do they
and do we similarly heed Beatrice's call to "y-tourn"? Do we hear her
call, and turn to look at her as she rises up on chains and pulleys, or
do we merely see the player who rises up? Or is the very question
that seeks an either/or itself misguided? The passage through gloom,
delimitation, separation and "flix" (line 100) is apparently not left
behind, but is rather brought into the final bidding and feasting.
Our miserable false concepts and delimitations, which we mistake
for the real, are the very shape of "[o]ure kyndes' Falle" (line 4528),
which we cannot but pass through, repeatedly falling back into
our occlusions and enclosures, and falsely extensive asymptotes.

It is almost as if our occlusions are a concealed miracle: a sum-
mons, to which Goobet, Thomas, God, the marvellous women, and
all of us as bystanders and wayfarers, offer a response, opening
the way for further responses. Through this "Rakelnesse, | All
rukelen" (lines 108-9), our being reconciled (as we must be) to
the going away and returning, our knowing of things is presented
as our highest kinship: "intellectioun is | Akyn to grace," says
Goobet, with his characteristically disarming directness (lines
2774-75). Human knowing is a redemptive binding, to which we
as both spectators and participants, in our very watching of the
play, perforce contribute: "We are entryng | Godd's perpetuall |
Retorn to Him-self | Goddfullyche" (lines 2651-53). In the same way,
human acts of knowing are akin to the relays and returns of the
cyclical dance, a "salvific compensacioun | for the . . . discreteness
of things" (lines 2017-19). This kinship pertains not just to human
beings exercising reason, but to all elements of reality: all that is

solid and all that is aerial yearns for "mutuall embraces, | On the singular poynt of Cryste" (lines 612-13). This does not betoken a triumphalistic or dogmatic certainty of knowing. Indeed, Goobet reminds Margaret and Anne of the prevailing uncertainty that surrounds all instances of knowing, and the dangers of sorcery and unbinding which lurk at all times either in loose words, or in overly confined words: for words are not nothing; they are part of reality's panoply. Nonetheless, no mistaken word or turn has the final word, as it were: there is always another attempt, another word which may bring forgiveness or redemptive dilation, a further step to be taken. The turning and mutual glancing of the final dance takes up every remote dispersal into its spheres, every inclement raindrop falling through the firmament, every teardrop, even the wide sea and ocean, from the height of Cassiopeia (line 4470) reaching through the universe, embracing both the living and the dead, the manifold, leaving nothing behind, not even a "sprekle of dowst" (line 910).

And yet, this ultimate manifold, this unending circular parade – not this time a parade of kings, but of all of reality – which no teller will foreclose, turns upon a singular point, on the most local punctiliar particular or singular, as to suggest a coincidence of unity and difference, of rest and motion, of sorrow and joy, of the knower and what is known. It has no extrinsic audience because the players – we all – are entailed in the game. The ultimate complexity and inscrutability appears oddly reminiscent of the village green, of our daily encounters, of the murky and the exalted alike. God, around whom all circles, seems one and the same with the performance which goes out and returns into the whirling orbit of the persons of the Trinity, into whose exchanges we enter in the same way that we are entailed in the encounters of the play – indeed, "Our 'three' is al-so | 'ffour' and 'ffive'!" And so, finally, Goobet is vindicated: the cosmic journey from rusticity to sublimity never took leave of the local grassy knoll. Beyond the discursive debates of the learned and lettered lies the "seeing all at once" of the peasant God, as contingent as He is necessary, as particular as He is universal; and so, perhaps, bound one day to arrive amongst us as we go about our daily round.

A NOTE ON MANUSCRIPTS
OF *THE BUMPKIN PLAY*

PLACE & DATE OF DISCOVERY (WHERE THIS IS KNOWN)	CONVENTIONAL NAME, TYPICAL FEATURES, & LISTING
Eighteenth Century Miscellany	*Crozier Manuscript* Fabula Rustici FR M. a. 172
Unnamed Hotel, Sidmouth Esplanade [c. 1977?]	*Crozier II MS* D. a l. 1554
Emmanuel College, Cambridge Foolscap box-file Feast of St Michael and All Angels, 1995	*Blotting Paper MS* Shorter, ends with divine *exitus* C. P. Mn. I. 17, c. 46r.
As above, Emm. Coll., Cambridge	*Pink ties MS* Hand-written version, pink string, miscellaneous food stains C. P. Mn. I. 18, c. 46r.
As above, Emm. Coll., Cambridge	Unbound fragments C. P. Mn. I. 19, c. 46r.
Emmanuel College Porters' Lodge Delivered by hand by unnamed person 25 November 1995	*Pigeon hole MS* Islay textual variant C. P. Mn.I.20, c. 46r.

PLACE & DATE OF DISCOVERY (WHERE THIS IS KNOWN)	CONVENTIONAL NAME, TYPICAL FEATURES, & LISTING
Unspecified public garden 1 December 1995	*Public Garden MS* C. P. Mc. I. 18, c. 46r.
Museum of College Life, Emm. Coll., Cambridge 15 February 1999	*Floorboard MS* Most elaborated version C. P. Mc. I. 21, c. 46r.
c. 2 January 2003	*Highbury MS* [separate textual tradition?] In private ownership C. P. Mn. I. 23, c. 46r.
Center of Theological Inquiry Date unknown	*Princeton MS* In private ownership
Bogotá, Colombia c. June 2022	*Bus Shelter MS* [not unlike Pink Ties MS?] In private ownership
Chiang Mai, Thailand 4–5 December 2024	*Chiang Mai MS* In private ownership

ACKNOWLEDGEMENTS

FINALLY, A NOTE OF THANKS TO ANNABEL LEE for her cover design, manicules, rabbicules, and the rendering of the diagram at *Fygure 1*; to Lida Cardozo Kindersley for her discerning typographical eye, and to Jacqueline Tasioulas for her exacting orthographic eye. To John Riess, Michael Schrauzer, the anonymous reviewers of Angelico Press, and to Tabitha Tuckett, Jane Wallace, and above all, to Thomas Harrison: *thank you thank you!* Thank you to Elise Morrison and Michael Wilcher for their work in preparing the index, and to Peter Harland for facilitating their work. I am grateful to four institutions for their custodianship of this play's tradition: the Faculty of Divinity, Cambridge, and especially the members of the 'D' Society; the Master and Fellows of Emmanuel College, and of St Catharine's College, Cambridge, and to the friars of the Priory of the Dominican Order in Cambridge, past and present. Thank you to the many helpers, invisible hands, archivists, players and readers who over the years have contributed to this play's continued life: Blake Allen, Silvianne Aspray-Bürki, Hjördis Becker-Lindenthal, Ragnar Mogård Bergem, Matthew Bullimore, Andrew Davison, Victor Emma-Adamah, Valentin Gerlier, Anatole Gibbon, Sepp Gumbrecht, Ruby Guyatt, James Hawkey, Joshua Heath, the late and beloved John Hughes, Robin Kirkpatrick, Simone Kotva, Andrew Lenox-Conyngham, Elise Morrison, Arabella Milbank, John Milbank, Vittorio Montemaggi, Simon Oliver, Adrian Pabst, Simon Ravenscroft, Albert Robertson OP, Andrew Sackin-Poll, Jacob Sherman, Janet Soskice, Steven Toussaint, Tony Street, Alain Tschudin, Heather Webb, Dominic White OP, Michael Wilcher, Rowan Williams and Mary-Jane Rubenstein. And to Flora, Freddie and Alexander who know that "Love is all we haue | On this rownde erth," y-wis. And to Don Cupitt, who died just as this edition was going to press, whom I miss very much. And to the countless many others who have read, enacted and bequeathed this play to us.

FABULA RUSTICI

A plaiye for All Sowles

The Guild of All Souls Playe
(pray for my soul!) [27]

FOL. IR

DRAMATIS PERSONÆ

DEUS (*wearing a ciclatoun cloke of crimsoun veluet wyth lyons of gold*)[28]

GOOBET-ON-THE-GREEN (A COUNTRY BUMPKIN, *wearing a blew
cote powdred wyth yellow flowre & blew semid with red, not so playne*)

S. THOMAS (ANGELIC DOCTOR)

JACQUES (A DOUBTER, *in crymson neckerchief*)

CHARLIE [*or* CHARLENE] HANDYMAN
[*or* HANDYVYMAN] (A PRAGMATIST, *wearing toolbelt*)

SOLEMN THEORETICIAN

HAPPY PILGRIM (*carrying the* HOLY BOOK)

MR NO-NONSENSE (A FREYND OF ALL)

MARGARET, PHILOSOPHE AND POETE

ANNE, PHILOSOPHE AND FFREYND OF LEYBNYZ

WIFE OF BATH (A FLEETYNG APPEARAUNCE, *red-stockynged*)

*Four drunken trybesmen,
    dysgysedly aparailed*

WEASEL

RAT

FOX

STOAT

Four mystical wymen

DIOTIMA

S. MACRINA

S. MONICA (*with kerchief*)

BEATRICE

PROLOGUE

[SCENE. *Upon a mede, Impyngton vilage Grene*]²⁹

GOBET-ON-THE-GREEN³⁰ [*equitando*]:³¹
Al-heil,³² al-heill,*   *all hail!
  Every maner of man,³³
5   For here am I,
  A carlysche* am!   *rustic gentleman
Lordings Hulsean,³⁴
  Clerkes and grad,
Sylens your din,*   *do quieten down!
10   And herken well!
For gracious Godd
  Groundyd* of all Godnesse,   *grounded in, or founded upon
As his grete glorie*   *great glory
  Never bi-gynning hadde,*   *is without beginning
15   And nought is but He,
  So does succour and save
All those that waxen abaished!*   *become perplexed
  And miraclis does werk,
As thawing fot-maidens,*   *maidservants
20   And trudging gigants!³⁵

Now lysteneth
  To our talkynge,
Abydyn sylens
  Stylle and sad,
25   For we purpos us
  Pertly styll,
In this wintry place,
  Thee pepyl to plese
With pleys ful glad;³⁶
30   Now lysteneth wel*   *listen carefully
In buxumnesse,
  Bothe more and lesse

Sothfastednesse,
Beweren newefangelnesse,
35 Gentyllys and yemanry,*   *company of refined and free-born
Yf blisful lyf
Lad this tyde;*   *if we are to have a good time
We xal* thou shewe,   *shall
As that we kan,
40 How that TRUTH
First be-gan.

Now, Saints awey
Are from us gone,[37]
And all their companye;
45 All Souls,
Through Godes* grace,   *God's [own]
Are throngyng fast,
To shewe us now
Our teme* at last.   *theme

50 For Soul is in a manere
All thynges![38]
Whiche is to say,
It's trewth that sings![39]

My name is
55 Gobet-on-the-greene,
And I am a burly
Heturly* bumpkeen*   *eager * bumpkin
Who gazes at the Mone.*[40]   *Moon
But yf the *soule is*
60 *In al thyng,*[41]   *all things
Then Trewth's in me,
Ferly to sen!*   *what a marvel to see!

How this wil be,
I xal sormise.*   *surmise
65 And ben ther-boute,
To ask the lads
That have some clout!

ACT ONE
SCENE 1

[GOOBET *wandering around the Village Green.* Enter JACQUES *whistlynge to hymself*]

JACQUES:

70   Whom do you seek?[42]

GOOBET:

Jacques, I seke you![43]
  You're a ful fetys* fellowe,   *very elegant
Floytynge, I hasard,
75   And will not quook*   *quake
Yf I maken questioun.
  Could you telle me,
What is truth?[44]

JACQUES:

80   That sownds, I must saye,
    More Pilate than *pilates.*[45]
I refuse its possibilitee,
    Goobet. [*scratching head*][46]
*Realte** isn't reale;   *reality
85   It notes not
Nociouns of trewth.
  Vraiment,
There are
  Whilende* trewths   *temporary
90 Of transitorie
  Fflottys-fact,
But these do not aryse
  Accordyng to
The trewth,
95   In the sense of
A coherent logick,

Nor of inklings
Of ynkerly*   *particularly
Yncky* ynwyt.*   *inky *understanding
100   *All is flix,*   *flux
Lattly* y-grasped,   *belatedly
As it al-wey al-redy
Aeirily eludes us.

GOOBET:
105   Oh deare, does that meane
That oonly routhelees
Randomness and
Rakelnesse,*   *rashness
All rukelen,*   *all heaped up
110   Are reale?
O whatt a rowten!*   *a great noise, a bellowing, a snoring
That does seeme
Dreich and drear!*   *dreary and bleak, especially of weather
How one must sureli
115   Rouken* and rounen!*   *cower down *talk secretly, whisper

JACQUES:
Yes, I suppose so.
Is it too annichilhatyng*   *annihilating
For a symple-hertid
120   Lumpen ladde
Lyke you?
But I get furls of francs⁴⁷
For waxyng so wysliche.*   *wisely

GOOBET:
125   Yes it is, I fear frigtilike,*   *timidly
And feblenly.*   *in weak or sorry fashion
And you'll get
Not a farthyng from me,
Never mynd a furl of francs.
130   Whoever obled* you   *offered oblation

Your obeley obols
   Must have obout-ga*   *gone about
And polle* the poraille*   *gained money by extortion *poor people
   As a post-truth pokke,*   *pustule
135 To lean on the least,
   In leasing* and leccherye.*   *falsehood *lewdness
Or is that just fake news?

JACQUES:
Er, um . . . .
140   I do not vnderstond
The recent reel
   Of global galavants.
I am gaye and gladde
   To have left them fynaly
145 In Purgatorie,
   Whose indeterminacy
Suits me down
   To the *Ungrund,*
And whose torture
150   Gilles is teachynge me
To make Masochian.[48]
   So why not go and speake
To my ffrende
   Charlie the Handiman?
155 He doesn't disagree with me
   Altogethyr;
In fact, he elaboraytes
   On whatt I say,
In his homespunne
160   Anglo-Saxon mannere.
Though a sensible liberal
   Campus fellow,
He hadde an inkling
   A whyle ago
165 That the werking pepyl

Might decyde
That yokels lyke me
Were out of touche.   [*et exit equitando*]

[*enter* CHARLIE THE HANDY[VY]MAN, *wearynge tool-belt
and wieldinge a truncheoun*]

170   GOOBET:
You look lyke
    You mean businesse,
And are a
    Practykal Puck.
175   Could you telle me,
    What is truth?

CHARLIE:
Yes, dear man!
    I, like Jacques,
180   Think treuwth
    As *correspondence to realite*
Is either *unadveylable**   *unavailable
    Or *meaninglesse*;
But do not worry,
185   Because truth bilongs
More curteisly
    To practykal, and not
Theoretical businesse.
    Sufficient treuwth
190   For human purpose
    Is advaileable
In the *successful attaynment*
    Of humanly sought endes
And *practykal contryvaunces.**   *contrivances
195   All this nonsense about
The truth of randomness —
    It is not my sort of thing *at all*,
And gets us Sensible Thinkers

Into rakish repute.
200 Yf we juste staye close
   To *whatt works by daye,*
Then we can do
   Anything we like
By night—
205 Wild but harmless things,
Like literary theory.
   While ordinarie folk
Jogelen* themselves   *entertain by jesting, performing tricks
   In vysual stupefaction,
210 We will get into
   Farre fewer fylan.*   *foulings

GOOBET:
Oh, I see.
   But, taryen—*   *tarry for a moment
215 This means that
   Truth is seruile   *servile
To fleetynge
   And contyngent
Trotevales!   *trifling things
220 Truew things
May be truew
   For a certeyn tyme,
But is that al,
   Tymen?*   *to betide, happen
225 We are now
   In the midst
Of the third
   Industrial revolucioun.
Digitall and Roboticch trewth
230   Is scant anything
I want to recunisse;*   *recognise
   It has oonly
Slydyrnesse* and sleythe,*   *slipperiness *trickery

Like Jacques's literarie stuffe.
235 No wonder everi-one
Is now sayinge
Any-wat thyng they want.
Is this speech so free?
It is certaynley *slipperyie.*
240 I can see the honest veracitie
Of your craftid carpentri,
Charlie,
But not of the latest
Titillating Twitterings,
245 Themselves tycen*   *enticed, or provoked
From Twitter Inc. HQ
In San Franciscu!
Bird-feed,
I dub them!
250 *Too-whit! too-whoo!*
And on top of that,
Yf the oonly mesure
Of the trewth of a practice
Were its success,
255 In the sense of
Wirken well,   *working or operating satisfactorily
Then, oh deare me,
Your kynd of truth
Is enterlich detached
260 *From the Good!*
An aueful lot of drasty*   *worthless, or trashy even
And draffen thynges*   *draff- or dreg-like things
Wirken curteisely*   *courteously or well
But lend no flouring withal.*   *flowering or flourishing
265 By this measure,
A Hoover[49] is truth,
A Hoover bagg,
And my granny's tin of string

        Labelled, "too short to use."

270   I'm not sure, Charlie,

        That I want you bothering

         To paint

        The door of my bothy,

         Or hammering it

275   Together agayn

         After wyld wyntry wederen,*   *exposure to adverse

        Yf you are going to   weather conditions

         Talke this tattling* tapinage;*   *loose talk *skulking

        It will seep and slike

280   Into your werk;

        It will teint it

         Most tawdrilie.

        And how do you descide

         When something is deemed

285   Successfyl or not?

         Tomorwe?

        Or the next daye?

         On an emty belly,

        Or a full one?

290   When you're blithe and glade,

        Or adoun in the dismol domps?

         I don't quyte see

        How your Theory of truth

         As non-theoretical,

295   Does not aefter all

         Thudden and Threngen

        Into Jacques's theory of truth

         As the enthronement

        Of te-tealte* randomness.   *unstable, or in jeopardy

300   [enter SOLEMN THEORETICIAN, *dismol-faced, head-tylting downwarde*]

CHARLIE:

Now looke here,
  Dear fellowe, [*addressing* GOOBET]
You're syly*   *silly, foolhardy
305   To be so down
On my idea of trewth,
  Bicause, as I see it,
It's *your oonly hope.*
  As an unlettrid bumpkin,
310   You haven't
Any alternative.[50]
I don't think you'll deliten in*   *delight in
  My frend,
Solemn Theoretician—

315   **SOLEMN THEORETICIAN:**
—You're a bumpkin, are you?

[*Cheeryng up at the presumed idiocie of others. Asyde*: ha! ha! ha!].[51]

I am traisten*   *confident, trusted
  In trewth in-wis,
320   Unlyke Charlie and Jacques.
  I bow down
Before the truth
  Of naturall science.
I'm not interested
325   In the success
Of its construccioun,
  But in whatt
Those operations
  Are held to un-hide,
330   *Out there*
  In solid realte.
Truth is an enterly
  Theoretical matter;
It is a propurte of the

335   *Way Things Are,*
     A mattere of hypotheses,
       Testyd by aspeccioun*   *observation
     And operacioun.*   *deeds, action
       It's thankfully in-dyfferaunt
340   To the *whimsical*
       Goodnesse of Things,
     And to their beauty
       And appreciacioun
     By human beyngs;
345   And to the waveryes
     Of our desyre
     And anymal
     Promptings of our will.
     Ahem!
350   This is why
     We need experts,
     And why the current
       Rejectioun of expertyse
     Is more than perilous.
355   I'm all for
     Solyd Facts,
       And Expert Boffins,
     In a Very Brittish Way.

GOOBET:
360   [*aside*: I don't mucch lyke this fellow!
       He seems a cold fyssh
     Who construwes without passioun!]
     I see. But in my view,
       It's a problem distinctyue of
365   Mucch naturall science
       That it will
     Hold something
       To be trewe
     Whiche seems rum to

370   Dong-hep* bothy-dwellers lyke me,   *dung-heap, ordinary,
       Yf they can grasp it at all, that is.   not at all fancy
       I worry that you
       Impose a goulf
       Betwyx my everydaye werld,
375   And the ironic gaze
       Of the scientific sage.
       Som-tymes science makes it seem
          As if whatt we see every daye
       Is but the same
380   As glimpsing faieries
       At the bottom of the gardeyn.
          Except the ordinarie wedes
       Are now the fayres,
          And some newefangled
385   Mathematik ghostes
          Are there after all,
       Yf you see whatt I mean.
          I believe that this is called
       "Phenomenalism."

390   SOLEMN THEORETICIAN:
       [aside: This Goobet is a rum bumpkin—]52

       GOOBET:
       And, while I mencioun it,
          Your idea of trewth
395   Is the property of an élite
          Whiche can vnderstond
       Those long enfilen*   *enthreadings
          Of infidele letters,
       Whiche mean nothing
400   To honeste rusticall folk.
       It seems to me
          A rather cold truth
       With lots of cheald*   *chilly
       Divisiouns

405 And sub-divisiouns,
    Bifore whiche
Society must abas yt-self.
    Whaht can it do,
But allow its gardeins*   *guardians
410   To ytake *vital decisiouns*
Whiche the rest of us
    Cannot comprehend?
While all we may do
    Is heven* oure-selfs abowt   *heave
415 With gruntyngis grislic!*   *horrible grunting

SOLEMN THEORETICIAN:
Too right!
    We must not be post-trewth.
And avoyding the reule* of an   *rule
420   Unlered* majority means,   *unlettered
I am afeered to say,
    Humilliauce to
Peple lyke thee-self.   *[exit, laughing heartili]*[53]

[*enter* HAPPY PILGRIM]

425 GOOBET:
Whatt abowt you,
    Happy Pillegrim?
Do you knowe
    What trewth is?

430 HAPPY PILGRIM:
Yes. I am very certayne
    About Truth, [*waving Holy Booke*]
And I much dis-lyke
    These haughty pepyl
435 Who are scepticall abowte truth,
    Like Jacques and Charlie.
I ytake refuge
    In the nocioun

That there is
440   Onther* Source   *another
Of Truth
    En-shrined in writ,*   *written sources
Practyces and traditiouns.

GOOBET: F. V 9
445 Hmmm, but is that not
    A bit ironyc?
Bicause for these sources
    And traditiouns
To acquere
450   Holful Authoritee,
Out-with the operaciouns
    Of human reasoun,
They must be regardid
    Quyte positivisticallie,
455 In a fashioun whiche semblaunces
    Scientific positivism it-self?
Swich an appeal to tradicioun
    Is nowadayes
Tourning quite atavistic
460   For that very reasoun,
Is yt not?
    Pople say things like,
"Let's stick to
    What is English,"
465 And that yncludes religioun,
    Never mynd whether
It is TRUEW,
    In Capytall Lettres,
Or it is not.
470   So isn't yours just trewth
In lower case lettres?
    It offers a
Paisaunt positivism

Whiche maybe you fancy
475   Will ytake in
A dong-hep personn lyke me,
Un-able to knoue any bettere?
But we're a bit
Wilier than that,
480   On the Grene.
I'm not so sure
I like the ydea
Of a bifurcatioun
Betwyx a werld of causes,
485   Knouen to science,
And a werld of
Ancestral meanynges,
Whiche are simpellie
The fantasies
490   Withinne our heads,
How-so-ever hallewen*   *hallowed
By local tyme.
Are you not
A dreame pillegrim,*   *pilgrim
495   Doomed to pursue
A *will o' the wisp*?

[*exit* HAPPY PILGRIM *feelinge aggrieyved*]

What a tricky situatioun this is.
With swich merkeful* alternatives,   *gloomy
500   I think I'd like to serch
For some better nociouns.
What I need, sureli,
Is to fynd
A theory of truth
505   Whiche *does not enthrone**   *enthrone
The random,
Is both theoretical and makable,[54]

*Both contemplatable and yhernandlike,**   *desirable
  *A mattere of feith**   *faith
510 *As well as resoun;**   *reason
    At home in
    Internationall
    Transitionall places,
  Like airport terminals,
515   But al-so here and nowe,
  On the grasy Green;
    And amenable
  To the *simplest apprehensioun,*
    (Bicause I am, after all,
520 A mere bumpkeen),
    As well as to *profound*
  And learnid elaboracioun?

ACT ONE
SCENE 2

[enter GOOBET, *with his goode ffrendys* MARGARET *and* ANNE]

GOOBET:

525   O Margaret,

      O Anne,

    Wher ben thee?

      The night is darke,

    And mirke* stille,   *lacking light, murky

530   For that these snirt and mirky* menn,   *stern and gloomy

    Who cal them-seilves lettred,

      Have made mee

    Ful of wiste*   *sadness

      And waimentrye:*   *sorrow and lamentation

535   Eyther the werld

      Is to be arraynéd flatte

    For their immateriall eye

      To falle vpon

    And commaunde;

540   Or els it slidens

    To nowght*   *naught, nothingness

      And we slither togedyr* with it,   *together

    In-to the gret dong-hep*   *a pile of manure, a great heap

      Of náhwar.*55   *nowhere

545   MARGARET:

    Ther must be

      Anothyr waye,

    In bitwyx

      These soylen

550   Tenebrose choyces!

      For creaytures,

    Smalle as attomes,*   *smallest unit of time

      Luculent* spangels,*   *shiny * ornamental tiny-ness

May ther bee,
555   In every wight*   *every one
A creayture's ymage in-betered.*   *hammered
Althouwgh they ar not
Suget* to oure sense,   *subject, subserviant
A werld may be namore*   *no bigger in size or degree
560   Than a grain, or tuppence.
Nature is corious,
And succh werks may shape,
Whicch our deflye* senses   *dull
Ethfully atscapen.*56   *escape easily
565   Each hidden thyng
Godde's autar* ys, y-wis,   *altar
Versing exchaunges
As ten-thusendfeld* elitropes,*   *thousand fold
                         * plants tending towards the Sun
In secrenese with eir.*   *air

570 GOOBET:
Yes, there is mucche
Thaht receydes,*   *recedes
Thatt we cannouwt* knoue.   *cannot
We cannought* be certeyn   *cannot
575 Eyther of som-thyng;*   *something
No lesse of no-thyng.*   *nothing
Nor ani-what incantacioun*   *magic, sorcery
Our wordes may unbinden
In speakynge thus.

580 MARGARET:
What is some-
Or no-thing
When one thyng
Bicoms* another?   *becomes
585 Certeynty is
Parforce falsitee.
Ther is no thyng;
Yet no nott-thynge is!

How can bothe be treue?
590   Throwgh analogie and slidynge,
By degree and conformacioun.
   All poyntid attomes,
They to Fire ytourne;   *turn
   Which by their drinesse,
595   They so light and flottynge bicome: *floaty
   Above the rest do flye,
And make theiselves
   A Sunne.
Whicch by friendship of parts,
600   A wheele of Fire ygrowes,
Whych being sphaericall,
   In a round nocioun goes.⁵⁷

ANNE:
Al is affinitee.
605   Trewth is kinship
Of creatioun,
   A gostely cognacioun,
Tourning bitwyx
   Soliditee and aeyriyalitee,*   *airiness
610   Desyring to bettren
   Theyr one-ment
By mutuall embraces,⁵⁸
   On the singular poynt of Cryste.
The clerest waterr
615   Conteyns tiny stones;⁵⁹
Solyd cristals
   Spangeled,
May be yliquefiyd;
   The strengest substaunce
620   Is spyrytually transparaunt
   To liht.*   *light
Therr are oonly
   Thre Realitiees:

Godd,
625   Chryst, & Spirit,
And for Crittures,
   With Chryst
As Holy Pivott
   Vponn Whom
630   Al lif tournes.

[*Enter* THOMAS, *gloffinge a Pizza Napoletana;* MARGARET *and* ANNE *walk off togyther talkiynge loftily*] [60]

GOOBET:
Hello!
   Are you the Angelic doctor?

635   THOMAS:
Why yes,
   As a mattere of fact,
Wit thou forsoth,*   *know thou for a fact
   I am.
640   How can I be of helpe to you?

GOOBET:
Well, can you tell me—
   Where can I fynd truth?

THOMAS:
645   Are you quite sure
   I am the person to ask?
Aren't I just an olde-fashiouned
   Aristotelyan realist?
A lot of pepyl *say*
650   That swich realism
Is rather out of fashioun these dayes;
   The idea that our *thoughts*
Are in concorde
   With the way things
655   *Are in the world?*

GOOBET:
In-deed so.
  And they are right,
For how can we
660   *Check our knoueledge*
Agaynst the werld,
  In order to see if it
Corresponds with it?
  Is that whatt you *really* think?
665 Are you an olde-fashiouned
    Correspondaunce Theorist?
Yf I oonly know things
  By thinking them,
How can I *check up* on
670   Whether my thowghts*   *thoughts
Duly correspaund?
  I wold need another
Brayn to do that with!
  Or bettere still,
675 The standpoint
    Of an aungel,
To compare the
  Picture in my mind
With whatt goes on out there.
680   And then we'd need
An archangele
  To chekke the angele's
Chekking up.
  And a Seraphin to chekke his chekking,
685 And a Cherubin to chekke his.
  We'd have triangulacioun
To an infynytenesse
  Of dyvyne
Gouernmental vywers—*   *inspectors
690   Bifore you can say

"*Ows ya holy farver?*" —
    Afferming
    Giorgio Agamben's view
    Of dyvyne gouernemente
695 As a synyster
    Kafkaesque bureaucracy.[61]

THOMAS:
I'll leave that for you to dicyde.
    But don't ytake
700 Giorgio too ceryously —
    He hangs out in places likke
    Roma and *Venezia*:
      Not the real *Ytalia* at all.

GOOBET:
705 [*aside*: Poor confusid fellawe.
    I hadde better ask hym
    More about his ideas,
      Euen if just out of pity.]
    Please do tell me more, Thomas. [*with compacient tone*]

710 THOMAS:
[*aside*: This Goobet is a curious *rusticus!*]
    All right then.
    May I direkt you
    To the opening article
715 Of my recent *Quaestiones*
    Disputatae de Veritate? [*pointes to velum skinne*]

GOOBET:
Mmm . . . ah yes.[62] [*readyng thoughtfully*]
    *Videtur autem quod**   *it seems that
720 *Verum sit omnino**   *the true is exactly
      *idem quod ens.**[63]   *the same as being
    But, oh, is it not
      Straunge?
    You seem to bigyn your

725   *Disputatioun on Tryth*
        With a consideratioun
           Of the relacioun
        Of *Trewth to Beying.*[64]
           Swich a startyng-pointe
730   Wold make
           No sense at all
        For contemporanye
           Or future
        Theories of truth.

735   THOMAS:
        Oh ys it so? Why is that?

        GOOBET:
        Well, from whatt I gather,
           They wil tend to aginne*   *begin
740   With a questioun swich as
           'How does one knowe a Thing?'
        But, from the outset,
           You posen
        That one owghtn't
745   To *refer* truth to beiyng,
        As if it were at a
           Remove from existence;
        But rather to aske,
           What kynde of beinge
750   *Trewth and vnderstonding*
           Themselves possess?
        As if everithing were
           Slumbering with significance,
        Wayting oonly
755   *To be awaykened*
        By the touch of spirit. [...*pauses, musyneg, hand on chinne*...]
           *"Verum est id quod est"** —   *the truth is that which is
        Perhappes, then, you are not
           A correspondaunce theorist

760 In the modern sense of that term?
        Perchaunce there is
     Another kind
          Of correspondaunce,
     Where-by thowghts
765   In our myndes
     Are in accorde with the
        Ways thyngs are
     At the deepest level
        Of cosmic sympathy;
770 At a level not of epistemologee,
        But of *ontologee?*

THOMAS:
Yes, if you are right,
   Then it must follow
775 That to *know somethyng*
      Is not to be indifferaunt
   To the thyng
      That one knows,
   For both the beyng
780   Of the thyng known,
   And the being
      Of the knower
   ....Will be affected.

                                              FOL. V 12

785 GOOBET:
   What a gladsom thowght!

THOMAS:
Yes, you see,
   It is so truew!
790 You vnderstond me very wel
      For an hyperborean *rusticus.**   *bumpkin, rustic "boor"
   In-wis, I begyn by askyng
      Abowt trewth
   As *a mode of existence.*

795   Just as that other
Middel-erth thynker,
  Aurelius Augustinus, once sayd,
Thynking is an
  Higher kynd of lif.[65]

800   GOOBET:
Ah, but you are not
  Wantinge to posen
That trewth is a particuler
  Kynd of beyng, are you,
805   Stalkin' the Grene
  In a spinnee-napron?*   *apron

THOMAS:
Great Hefnis, no!
  Trewth is noht
810   A kynd of beyng;
  As a transcendentall,
It is conuertible with Beyng,
  With whiche it has
An absolute resonaunce...

815   GOOBET:
...in the entirety of both terms?[66]
  Trewth is open to Beyng,
Like my new pony-and-carte,
  Conuertible with the air?
820   Dispyte all the
  Gret rein and mudde,
And slipperinesse,
  We have got conuertibles
Even 'ere you knoue.

825   THOMAS:
Yes, but oonly if it is an
  Openn-rof Ferrari,
Or Alfa-Romeo, at a pinche...

GOOBET:

830 [*Aside*: Forsooth! He is a prophett as well as a doctore!]
But how can trewth
  Be lyke a cart
Or mouable wagon?[67]
  My pony-and-car
835 Is openn to the eir,
  But it is noght one-weld
With the air yt-self;
  It cannot ytake flight
Like a byrd.

840 THOMAS:
My deare fellowe,
  "Conuertibility"
Is fondamental
  To our middle-erth
845 Traditioun of Neoplatonysed
  Aristotelianism.
Everi-thyng that exists
  Can be sayde
To be *unified*,
850   *Good, Truew* and to be *a thyng*,
And also *som-thyng*.
  For many, al-so,
All that exists
  Is *bewteowse*.*   *beautiful, beauteous
855 At least, that is trew
  In the Meridionall.
Else-wher, I'm not so sure...
  Though Parys was
Not so badde.
860   Yf a *som-thyng*
That is *trewe*
  Is also *goode*, for exaumple,
Then *som-thyng-ness*,
  Whiche we learnid clerkes calle

865   *Aliquid,**   *anybody, anything
       Must "convert" with the
       Good and the trewe.
       For this theory,
       Accordyng to my own acompt,*   *account
870   Beyng is the
       Focal transcendentall,
          Bicause som-thyng
       Must exist
          Bifore it can be
875   Ani-thyng else.
          Beynge is so supreme
       That it is biyonde
          Even the ydea
       Of the highest
880   Created rank,
       And biyond the ydeas
          Of more or lesse,
       Even though it is
          At one
885   With the highest
          Uncreated realite—
       This is som-thyng
          That I am gathering
       A few scholars in
890   A place called Oxnaforda,
       On a mythical eit-lond*   *island
          Other-quar* biyond   *somewhere else
       The hauen of Caleis
          —a mysty place,
895   Iust like here— [*lookyng about suspeciouslye*]
          With its own Mesopotamia,[68]
       Do not quyte vnderstond,
          As they are ledd
       By Signore Ibn Sina.
900   Still, *beying as created,*

As whatt I distynguish
   As *ens commune*,*   *common being
In wis,* lies biyond   *in truth
   All hierarchicall qualificatiouns,
905   And is equaly close
   To every level
Of the metaphisicall ierarchy,
   Bicause an archaungel
And an ant,
910   And a sprekle of dowst,*   *speck of dust
Even a bumpkin
   From once barbarin londs,
Al these thyngs
   Equally exist.
915   As the obscur author
   Of *Liber de Causis* once sayde,
The fyrst and
   Most emynent cause
Is curyously mooste intymate,
920   And the mooste contubernyal.*[69]   *friendly, companionable

GOOBET:
So, you mean that *esse*
   Is equaly close to
Genus, species,
925   Substaunce and accident?

THOMAS:
Incredibile!
   You are but an
Humble cottar!
930   I can see that there is
No-thyng to enbesy* your-self with   *busy
   On cold fennyland euenyngs*   *evenings
But to read
   Learnid manuscripts...
935   And that here the

Learnid has seeypid*   *seeped
Into the vulgare,*   *vernacular tongue
  Or ys it
The other wey
940   Arownd?
Yes, you are right:
  An accident, per exaumple,
May be less self-staunding
  Than a substaunce,
945 But it juste as mucche *exists*,
  As does a substaunce.[70]

GOOBET:

When one seiz* that trewth   *says
  Is convertible with Beyng,
950 One is saying that trewth,
  Like Beyng,
Shatters the usual ierarch*   *hierarchy
  Of categoriall priorities,
In swich a way that   *such
955   The humblest creatur
Equally shines with the
  One light of trewth,
As the mooste exaltid,
  The most sublimated,
960 And is just as
  Revealing of it.

THOMAS:

Yes, that's right.
  For an humble bumpkin,
965 Albeit one with
  Aspiratiouns to wysdoum
Biyond his estate,
  I expect that's quyt
Reassuring news?

970   [GOOBET *in grete murth, but nowght to forget his God*]

ACT ONE
SCENE 3

[*in whiche* GOOBET *and* THOMAS *walke abuwt The Green*]

GOOBET:
So, Trewth is convertyble
  With Beiyng.

975   But if that is the case,
  Why does one need to *adde*
Truth to Beiyng?
  Why do we give them
Differaunt names,

980   As we do a fox gloue*   *foxglove
And shepherd's purce,*[71]   *purse
  Whiche are dyfferent
Heggerow flouers?*[72]   *hedgerow flowers
  Why can we not

985   "Disquote" trewth,
  Like the new
Anglo-Saxon doctores?[73]
  And why do we not fitten
A styll modishly

990   Minimalyst sleight* here?   *strategy
After al, the fox gloue
  And shepherd's purs,
And al other iblouens,*   *blooms
  Are just "ther-rightes,"* *right there [in space or time]

995   Are they not?
  To say that
"*It is true that*
  Swich flouers are ther-rightes,"
Is it chauncefulliche* juste a   *perhaps, chance-fully

1000   Verbale longe-hande
For the bodiliche gestur*   *gesture

Of pointinge to theim-self?

[GOOBET *poynts to some shepherd's purse by the wey-seide*]

THOMAS:

1005   Good questioun, Goobet.
     There are seuerall reasouns,
   All relayting to the
     Waye in whiche we see thyngs
   From our perspectif
1010   Of situated-nesse
   And sondernesse.*[74]   *diversity
     It is bicause of oure
   Finite *modus* of comprehendinge
     That we see Beyng
1015   *Vnder differaunt aspects.*

GOOBET:

Oh deere. I'm not
   Quyte vndoutous*   *undoubting, certain
Thaht I vnderstond
1020   All this talke of *modus.*
   Yt does sounde too unkyndly
     For the vernacular treueth
   Of Kyndenesse
     To whiche
1025   I am mucche attacched
     From birth, naturely.

THOMAS:

For sothly.
   Well, let me say that your
1030   Raw rustik jargoun
     Must have its
   Own complexities,
     Sutilties and purteynings
   Whiche overpleien*   *outplay or defeat
1035   My plain Latyn burthen,

Even though oure
  Apparaunt *claritas*
Can shyne with the
  Proliferating analogicall lightes
1040 Of al its many realizatiouns!
  Lyke the word
Clarity it-self.
  I fere that those
Oxenford types[75]
1045   May be foryetting
Their natif
  Wit of assonance,
And the mijst hakel* of   *mantle of mist
  Bedazzlement,
1050 Whiche aparenly
  Latyn blasenesse*   *glistening brightness
May forhiden* in its very   *conceal
  Sharpshipe of figuracioun!
The Latin mode
1055   Is not naturall
To those barbarine-boren,
  And there is rather
An affynity of contraryes,
  For its true exponents,
1060 With one swich as you.
  But I digresse,
As is *not* my wont!
  It is the effect of this
Clammy fogge
1065   Al abowt me—
In whiche terrayn did you
  Say we reside?
Vnder whose jurisdictioun?
  But 'tis no mattere.

1070 Let me explain.
  Accordyng to one of these

Aspectes of Beiyng
(That described
By the term
1075   "Being" yt-self),
The thyngs whiche we bihold
Seme to us to be
Discrete,
To *lenger**   *reside, linger (secretly)
1080   *In them-selves.*
Being is,
As we have juste sayd,
Equaly close to al-thynges,
Genus and species, and so forth.
1085   Bicause of this,
Existence seems to have a
A priuate nextnesse
And propinquite
To eacch thyng,
1090   Or aqweyntyng,*   *fellowship
And it follows from this
That things theim-self
Remein priuate
To theim-self,
1095   Haue a certayn
Self-identicall treueship*   *integrity
Whiche spryngs reversely
From the treweshipe*   *integrity
Of relatedness
1100   To the originall principle,
Beyng yt-self:
*Esse ipsum,**   *Being itself
*Quid est Deus.**[76]   *which is God

GOOBET:
1105   Yes, I see whatt you mene.
I oftyn notis that

Superabundable relatednesse
   Whenne I am out on the Grene.
Thyngs remaiyn
1110   In a discrete quietude,
Distingt from one an-owther,
   Thouwgh all is evenly sonne-liht
In the glode,*   *evenly sun-lit in the glade
   And in som sense
1115   Self-absorpt,
   As if reverberatyng
In theyr own elumining
   And gletering.*   *shining or glittering

THOMAS:
1120   So, you are a powet* too,   *poet
   Like your Englisshe Chaucer,
Who has rhymed
   In his barbaryus tonge
The lewd and bawdy tales
1125   Of our Boccaccio,
Yet is withal, it seems,
   Not without wit,
Courteisie and the pietee
   Suityd to a courteour...
1130   But that's not
   The oonly way
In whych things
   Shew them-selves to us,
Euen on the Green,
1135   My deare Gobet.

GOOBET:
Is it not?

THOMAS: FOL. I5 R
No; thyngs do not
1140   Always seme

To relate to heim-selves
   Al-one.
Som-whiles—
   In fact, offtyn-tymes—
1145   Things appear,
   Acordyng to our
   Modus cognoscendi,
    Our bias of vnderstonding,
To *relate*
1150   *To one an-other.*[77]

GOOBET:
You mean,
   Like you and me
Here in our discussioun?

1155   THOMAS:
Yis. You see,
   Beings all-so
Relate to each other
   By *moving outwardes*
1160   *From theim-selves,*
   In communicatioun,
By expressive accioun,*   *action
   And to-wardes their own
Fynall* eends   *final
1165   Of self-realisatioun.
The seconde—moving—
   Aspecte of thyngs,
Follwyng vpon their
   Mere inert beiyng,
1170   Reacches its ovemest* pitch   *highest
   In the accioun
Of the muynde*   *mind
   As vnderstonding truth.
The thridell,* yet more exstatic   *third
1175   And teleologicall aspect,

Is realysed in Lif,*   *life
And concerns
The good of
Those thynges
1180   Wherthurgh they are lynked
With other thinges,
And fynd their
Proper stonding-place*   *standing-place
In the order of thynges.[78]
1185   For spirituall creatures,
This is wyll and desir,
Their longinge.
Sometymes, accordyngly,
I have sprecende of
1190   Three acts:
Existyng,
Mouinge outwardes, and
Mouinge towardes an ende.

In the case of humanyte,
1195   Arte and thowght
Move outwardes,
Wher-as etikall* behaviour   *ethical
Moves outwardes
Towards a gol,
1200   Euen though it is
This acte
Whiche realises
Human nature,
And so by outher wey,*   *in another way
1205   It remains wholly inwarde,
As Simone Weil,
Taking no notice of Heidegger,
Will one daye animadvert.

GOOBET:
1210   Goodnesse.

THOMAS:
In the case of the human
  Secunde acte,
The activitee of knoueing,
1215   Dyfferent muchel-wat* bicome   *things
Newly related,
  By ben situated
Withinne each other,
  Or being assymilated
1220 To one another.
  This is a relatiounshipp of
Convenientia,
  Of *economically fittyng*
And hovable*   *suitable, appropriate
1225   *Belongyng-together,*
An instance of anologie.[79]
  Evry beyng is
In this way
  Relayted to knoueledge,
1230 But some beyngs
  Are relayted to knowen
Oonly insofarre as
  They are knouen,
And noht as
1235   Theim-selves knouinge.

GOOBET:
How very curyus.
  Could one say
That the outmore*   *outer
1240   Relatioun of goodnesse
Is aspecyally realised
  In livyng creytures,
Lyke the conyngs*   *rabbits
  Hoppinge abowt The Grene,

1245 And the fayries flittynge
         To and fro in the eir,
      The waterr and the lond al-so;
         And the innere relatioun
      Whiche you mencioun
1250   Is mooste realysed
      In the living creatures
         Who are given
      To vnderstond,
         Lyke the solempne dons
1255 Squaring on King's Parade,[80]
         Whome we Fennish folkes*   *folk
      Try to bi-shun;*   *avoid
         *"oer sea"** we call it...   *overseas, abroad

THOMAS:
1260 Well, not exactly.
         For stille more aeriyal
      Is the exstasie
         Of our mynde's motion
      As will,
1265   Passing out beyond us
      To join the conynges*   *rabbits
         And *ninfae**   *nymphs
      In their rejoycing.

         And this
1270 Parayde of Kings
         Is an obscure school!

      Could it be
         That I have been abloyd*   *carried off
      In my dreams
1275   To the fabled
      Island of Thule,
         Other-wise namyd Albyon,
      Where lies now the

Lond of the Englisce?
1280   They are in-wis
Curiously renowned
For their learning—
Whether traced
To the Pythagorean lore
1285   Of the druid-masters,
I know not.
But their centris* of wisdom   *centre
Is Oxenford—
Yes, I know of it—
1290   Whiche is where our
Franciscan friar-brethren
Are brewing
Straunge nociouns,
To whiche I alluded,[81]
1295   And would sonder in twie*   *tear apart, sunder in two
The domains of
Theorycall and praktycall wisdom:
The inner
Unity of Thoughtes,
1300   And outer
Travelling of Wille,
Of whiche we have been
So earnestly speaking...

WIFE OF BATH:
1305   [entering in a fluster, red-stockynged, layden with overflowing
baskets; speakyng in scathing tone][82]
The lymytours and
Other hooly freres,
As thikke as motes*   *specks of dust
In the sonne-beam,
1310   Maketh that ther ben
No fayeryes!*[83]   *fairies
[rushes off, leaving a trail of cabbages and turnips strewn][84]

THOMAS:
The dame quod rightly!
1315   Ther walketh now,
A lymytour himself
    In undermeles* and in morwenyges*!85   *early part of
[*Aside*: How am I so suddenly at ease   the afternoon
    In their rough brogue?   *mornings

1320 But whatt a splendyd fellaw
    This Gobet is.
I might invite him to join
    My *Ordinary Disputatiouns*;
I do think the
1325   *School of The Green*
Surpasses this unknouen
    Parade of Kings . . .]

Now, of corse,
    This is not
1330 My owne
    Originall Thowghte.
But these thriple
    Ways of relatyng
Are Augustinyan
1335 Determinatiouns of Beyng
—*Being, Lijf, and Knouledge*—
    As enunciated in his treatise,
De Libero Arbitrio.
    I connyngly entangle
1340 These determinatiouns
    With the thowghts of
The Philosophe—
    Aristotle to you—
Rude unlettred lad.
1345   In-wis,
Augustyn hadde

A-redy integrated
The Philosophe's nocioun
That the lijfe
1350   In anymals
Senses it-self,
With the Stoic idea
That lijfe
All-ways seeks
1355   To sustain it-self
In its truew essence.
He calls this
"The inner sense,"
And vnderstonds
1360   Human reasoun
To be a further sensyng
Of this sense it-self.
This is why he thinks of
Resoun* as   *reason
1365   *A higher kynd of lijfe.*
In-wis, he was
Evry bit as fond
Of animalls as Aristotle was
—Even if—*ahem*—
1370   You may other-whiles*   *at one time or another
Have read otherr-wise.[86]

GOOBET:
I've just hadde a thowghte!
These threfold
1375   Augustinian determinatiouns
Are rounde as a cercle,
Like a roundelay or
Or Maypole daunce
Of fayre maeidens
1380   When somer ys icomen ben![87]
As a byinge,*   *being

A thynge remains in it-self;
As liffing,*   *living
  It opens it-self
1385 Throwgh the operatiouns of lijfe,
  Towardes others,
And perceiven that
  It does this;
And as knowen
1390   Or knowing,
It retourns from others
  To it-self,
Bi-cause it tells yt-self
  That it has been
1395 Rowndelling in a daunce!⁸⁸
  Animals know they are dauncing,
But humanyte can
  Name the daunce,
And, as it were,
1400   Stand above it
Like an aungel!

THOMAS:
You are a splendidious bumpken.

GOOBET:
1405 You are mest gentil.*   *most kind

THOMAS:
Not at all.
  So we have seen
Three aspects
1410   Of our *modus,*
And I like your ydde*   *idea
  Of a cercle
Or a daunce of graces.
  But, more misteriously stille,
1415 One might say

That this cercle
Traces the mediatiouns
Of *a further transcendental,*
Whiche is in hid*   *hidden, in hiding
1420   In being manyfest.

GOOBET:
Really? Ooo.
    A many mo?*[89]   *another one?
FOL. 25 V

1425   THOMAS:
Yes, the further transcendental[,]
    Whiche I have
Al-redy whispered[,]
    Is *Beuaute.**   *beauty
1430   I begyn to thinke
    She is trewly such-wat,
Now I realise
    That your reyny climes[90]
Make the grace*   *grass
1435   So grene,
Even at our Souling tyme.
    Treuly,
*Tota pulchra es,**[91]   *you are all beautiful
    And beuaute is
1440   Eauerihwer,*   *everywhere
    Like grace,
As for some resoun
    An obscure French *curé*
One daye declarynge.[92]
1445   Beaute bestows Herself
Oblikely*   *obliquely
    On each of these
Three stations.
    For She occasions
1450   All instances

Of economic harmony,
Fittyngness and proporcioun,
Includingly that betwix
Byinge and knouen,*   *being and knowing
1455   And byinge, knouen and
Goodnesse.
We cannot see
Beaute as such,
But we espy Her
1460   In everithyng.
She is closingli*   *inclusively
Invysible
And hyper-viseble.

GOOBET:
1465   Yes, I see.
Beauty is oblike
And euherwihere!
You cannot
Avoid her,
1470   But she's
Hard to cacche,
Like our
Local wenchis.
But how does
1475   Beauty *mediate*?
Rounde these parts,
She ben
A lot of troubull . . .

THOMAS:
1480   Fyrst of all,
In-so-muchel as Beyng
Is som-thyng whiche
Resides in it-self
By a kynd of treueship,*   *integrity
1485   Beauty is apparaunt

As the mesour*   *measure
  Of that treueshipe;*   *integrity
Secoundly, insofar as Beauty
  Is involved in the
1490 Manifestatioun of thyngs
  In thair trewship,*   *integrity
With-ought whiche
  There could be
No visibilitee,
1495   It is foundamental
To knouen;*   *knowing {that something is true}
  And, thriddely,
In-so-much as Beauty
  Is lynked with desyre,
1500 It is croucial
  To the ebbe,
Or outgoinges,
  Or exstasies
Of the wille
1505   And the Good.

GOOBET:
[*coyli, with a side-wayes looek . . .*]
Why is beautee
  Linked with desyr?
1510 I would have
  No ydea about that . . .

THOMAS:
The resoun is
  That Beauty
1515 Is that whiche
  Plesede the [eien]sight.

GOOBET:
Oh, I see.
  [*aside*: So endowyd with profunde lettrure, this doctour!]
1520 Fancy thaght!

THOMAS:
This role of Beauty—
  Though I have never
Expressed this directly,
1525   Bicause of my
Trans-Alpine doubts,
  Up until now,
Buoyed up by this
  Gobet of the Green,
1530   And his revelation
  Of the blythe North
—Is in some way importante
  To comprehendinge the character
Of my theory of vnderstonding.
1535   When I speke of a *proportio*
Betwyx Beyng, Knouen
  And Wylling
Of the Good
  —Rather than
1540   The more mechanycalle
  Methametik
Proportionalitas,
  Whych would dinote
A visible
1545   Mesurable ratio—
I am alluding
  To the ineffabele
Concorde betwyx
  The transcendentals,
1550   Whereby, in the
  Finyte worle,*   *world
Thyngs coincide,
  And yet appear
To be distingwid.*[93]   *distinguished

1555   GOOBET:
Oh! So, Truth shews
   Beauty
Through Herself,
   And the Good leads
1560   To the Treue.
   But we could not thurghloken*   *examine
These relatiouns
   As if at a
Mesurable distaunce.
1565   We have to maken a skip
Around the maipole
   In wodis and medowis*   *woods and meadows
For ourselves
   In search of Spring,
1570   Both milde and wilde,
   As for Edward Thomas,
After getting off his bike
   To read a bit of Coleridge.

THOMAS:
1575   Yes. And this
   Sense of some-thyng
Immanently disclosid
   Through som-thing ellis,
In an unmesurable wey,
1580   But in a facioun
Experyenced
   As harmonious,
Suggests an
   Aesthetic dimensioun
1585   To my theory of treuth.
   Evry jugement of treuwth
Is an aesthetic jugement,
   Though I am getting
Ahead of myself

1590   Into the Romantic epoch
        By suggesting this.[94]
            All the isame, it is true
        That a lay French doctor
            Is right to say that
1595   My visioun of realitee
            As analogical,
        Convenient
            And so beauteful,
        Is bound up with the
1600   Implicit priority
        Whiche I give to
            Existential jugement
        Over the formal
            Grasp of the concept
1605   Or nocioun.
            I am in-wis
        No Structuralist.

        We Ytailes* love the   *Italians
            Lijfe-filled philosophie
1610   Of the caffè
            And the chaumber,
        And tend to escheu
            The philosophie
        Of the scriptorium
1615   Or post-alchemical laboratory:
        Bones to Philosophie![95]

        GOOBET:
        How amasynge.
            I do not think those felawes*   *fellows
1620   I met earlier
            Would know whatt to say
        To all of this!
            They are not
        Much concerned with style.

1625   THOMAS:
        Yes, they were
            Dreary felowys.
        But in fact,
            Things are even
1630   Straunger still!
            This aesthetic
        Cercling of mediaciouns*   *encircling of mediations
            And analogical
        Out-guoings
1635   And retourns,
        Whiche links
            Al-thing together,
        Is an aspect of Being
            Whiche exists
1640   *In the Soul*
            (And supremely in
        The dyvyne spirit).⁹⁶

        GOOBET:
        Presumably,
1645   You do not tothinken by this
        That the Soul arrives
            Thus-wise
        As an after-thought,
            Th-wis, once the
1650   Priuate closeness
            Or nextnesse
        Of Being
            To distinct things
        Has been established?

1655   THOMAS:
        No. This is bicause
            These aspects of Byinge
        Do not unwinden
            Successiuelye.*   *do not unfold successively

1660   It is rathermor the case
      That these distingt muche-whatt*   *sundry things
    Simply would not
    Fully *be*
    Without the Soul's
1665   Knouing of theim.
    Therefore, the Soul,
      Whiche one might see
    As yet anouther
      Refractioun of Being,
1670   Is not there
      To *mirror* things,
    But is a primordiall
      Mode of Being,
    Revealing being
1675   As som-thyng
    Whiche is
      Alweis wel-governed,
    As a cosmic polity.
      For the soul,
1680   As Aristotle forn-seid,*   *previously mentioned
      Is the form of formys,*   *form of forms
    The heart of liflinesse,*   *animating force
      As the principle of nutriment,
    Movement and sensatioun.

1685   What this shews
      Is that evry
    Animal functioun
      Is also a delectacioun
    Or a sorrow;
1690   A valuation.
    Rabetts do not go hoppin
      About your Green
    Without eythyr
      Pleiingli,*   *in play, for fun

1695   Or bringen
       To gref.*   *coming to grief
     For I can smell
       Clop-stert, Whit-rat,*[97]   *Stoat and Rat
     And clever Fox
1700   Is never far away.[98]
     Bicause the rabetts
       Sense that they are sensing,
     They tell theim-selves,
       A-cordyng to al
1705   The ancient doctors,
       Including the Philosopher
     And Augustine Aurelius,
       That thynges are
     Eythyr good or bad.
1710   Syns creatures have sawles,*   *souls
     Erthily frum-scheft,*   *earthly creatures
       They live more intensely.
     In his treatise *De Anima*,
       The Philosopher says that
1715   True and false
       Are just a more
     Universalysed and stathele*   *stable
       Good and badde,
     Just as reasoun is a kynd of
1720   Redoubled feeling.
     His way of
       Being spyrytuele
     Was more mondaine
       Than your modern dons
1725   Seem to prefer—
       But, as a Neapolitan,
     I warm to his way
       Very much i-wis.

ACT TWO
SCENE 1

[*Still on The Green; enter* MR NO-NONSENSE, *lurking behind a bush, evesdroppyng and unaspied*]

1730   MR NO-NONSENSE:
[*aside*: Who are these
    Motle felauwys?*   *motley fellows
A bumpkin and a friar
    Eating pizza?]

1735   GOOBET:
Your Neapolitano ideas
    Of the Soul,
And assimulacioun*   *assimilation
    And adequation,
1740   Are very kyryous* i-wis.   *curious, strange
    They appear to offer
A realist conceptioun of trewth,
    But me-smells
A fume of idealism besydes?

1745   MR NO-NONSENSE:
[*aside, muttering and scandalised*: This plump friar
    Is no ordinary
Word correspondence theorist!
    I would *hate* to be
1750   Associated with him,
    And would certeinly
Naefre* be seen ded   *never
    Squaring with him
On the Parayde!
1755   What a lot of
Poppycock he spouts!]

THOMAS:
Yes, Goobet.
  Being is not
1760 Bifore knowing;
  So, if Being mesures
Knowledge,
  Knowledge
Equally mesures
1765 Being.

GOOBET:
One might call this
  "Ydealle* realism,"   *ideal
Then?

1770 MR NO-NONSENSE:
[*aside, turning bright redde, styil behind a boske of breres*: What?!!!]

THOMAS:
Yes, I suppose so.
  For bicause
Truth and Being
1775 Are conuertible,*   *convertible
On with anouther,
  There is contynuhede*   *continuity
Bittuhen* the way things are   *between
  In the phisical
1780 And bodily world,
  And the way muchel-wat are
In our muynde.*99   *mind
    [MR NO-NONSENSE *storms off in bewildered stupor*]

GOOBET:
1785 This "contynuhede"
  You speke of...
It is not a contynuhede
  In the sense of
A mirroring

1790   Or static reflecting
            Of our thowghts
              Simply being
            "Treue to the facts," is it?

THOMAS:
1795   No. It's more alich to*   *like
              A parallel
            Bitwix the
              Way thyngs are
            In materiall substaunce,
1800   And the way thyngs are
            In bodily sensatioun,
              And then endeli*   *finally
            In our myndes.
              The deduccioun of thoughts,
1805   In order to be true,
              Must ecco and reboundyth agen
            The declinsoun* of being   *declension [grammatical]
              Accordyng to an
            Emanative or outspringen
1810   Generacioun of the cathegories*   *categories
            That was but lurken
              In Aristotle,
            Bifore the *Book of Causes*
              And the letterly Persian
1815   Made it
              More apparaunt.[100]

            Knowing involves
              A real relacioun,
            Whereby one's thowght
1820   Occasiouns
            A teleological realisacioun
              Of the formality of thynges,
            And in doing so,
              Is itself

1825 Browght to fruicioun.
     For to know
Is to live
     More intensely,
To help the cosmos
1830 To be
What it ought
     To be;
To be its gardynere*   *gardener
     In-wis.

1835 GOOBET:
Do you mean to posen
     That the actuale
Thenking of thyngs*   *thinking of things
     Brings them to their *telos*,
1840 Like the tendyng of plauntes,
     An holie husbondrye?

THOMAS:
Yes. This happens bicause,
     In my oppynyon,
1845 Although trewth is
     Less properly in thyngs,
It is in wis
     In theim-self also;
It is, as it were,
1850 *A dormaunt power,*
Slomered*   *sleeping
     Untyl it comes
To be knouen,
     And in that selue moment,
1855 The power of its trewth
Is awakned
     Or animated.[101]
The oke tree
     Growing on the Grene,

1860   Whuch dureth long tyme,
       With hard rynde,
    Is true,
       But al sooth* still   *all true
    Is the oke tree I feel,
1865   And feel I am feeling.
    And truer styl
       Is the same tre
    That I realise
       I am feeling
1870   In the liht of the
       Devyne jugement;
    Or in other wordys,
       The oke tree that I
    Come to knoue.

1875   [MR NO-NONSENSE *returns, emboldened by a Fitzbillies Chelsea bun or wigge, interrupts* THOMAS *and* GOOBET]

FOL. 35 R

MR NO-NONSENSE:
    [*houtinge and quaveringe*]*   *shouting and trembling
    This is all poppycock;
1880   If we must talk in these
    Pompows* Continental terms   *pompous, pretentious
       (I'm a UKIP supportour
    Mi-self,
    AND PRUD OF IT!
1885   Unlike Solemn
       Theoretician, who,
    In this respect,
       Is a disappointment
    To me—
1890   I sorweyed* to see him   *sorrowed
    In that Dreaded Queue),[102]
       Beyng is just an
    Inclusive genus

Of that whych is simply
1895   Indifferently "ther-righte";
It is neuterall
As to quality
And parfitness,*103   *perfection
And my mind can
1900   Represent it.
And that's a fact.
Either som other-whatt is
Closyd in the pot o' cley
When one lifts the lid,
1905   Or it is not.
Cheddar chese, for exaumple,
Is eythyr ther-right,
Or it is not,
If my wif has
1910   Mynned to buy it
From Seynesbury's;
And whyther it is
Wolgal* mowse-trappe   *vulgar
Or a mature Stilton,
1915   Has nothing to do
With this particuler questioun.
And come to mencioun it,
My wif is either ther-rightes,* [*pointing*]   *over there
Or she is not,
1920   Just like chese!

THOMAS:
Please calm down
And have a slice of my pizza—
The chese is
1925   *Mozzarella di Bufala*,
By the way.
Let me see if
I understond you,

Though in trewth,
1930   I do not know
What a bare fact
Would look like.
It sounds to me
So soled*   *solid
1935   That it would
Have to be
Emty,
As an oracular voys* tells me,   *voice
One of your Sages of the Parade
1940   Will one daye say.
For yis! I see a
Straunge future
For that Parading School.
One daye, it will be
1945   Famows and modern,
And yet
Secrely arcane
And incloside;*   *enclosed
The very
1950   Opposyt of Oxenford,
Whiche will
Always seem
Medieval
But is already
1955   Modern,
And full of your
No-nonsense...

But whatt seems to be
Making you so angry and wroth,
1960   Mr No-Nonsense,
Is the idea of *knowing*
As a kind of
Ontological wakynnyng.   *awakening

MR NO-NONSENSE:

1965   Thank you for the pizza. [*slightly calmer*]
      Yes, whatt I have no toleraunce for
    Is the suggestioun
      That knouingal* is itself   *acquiring knowledge
    As much a
1970   Mode of beyng
    As the existence of materiel
      Or other-wyse
    Self-standyng substaunce.
      It seems fremeddlike ydiotic,*   *perfectly idiotic
1975   And daungerous even.

THOMAS:
Hmmmm;
    So you wold not
    Like the idea of
1980   *Esse intelligibile,*
    The idea of *thought as*
      Intentional existence,
    Building upponn Augustine's idea
      Of thowght
1985   As a "higher kind of lyfe,"
      An intensified animality?[104]

MR NO-NONSENSE:
Good gracius no. [*spluttering pizza*]
    This is more than I can staund.
1990   I have absolutely no ydea
      What you are talkinge abowt.
    [*sitting down and trying to recover*]

GOOBET:
[*addressing* THOMAS] Please can you and I
1995   Reassume our discussion?

THOMAS:
Yes.

GOOBET:
We hadde astahelede*   *established, settled
2000   That intellectioun
Is not an
    Yndifferent speculatioun;
It is a
    Comlich ratio*   *comely
2005 Whiche arises
    Itwix muchel-whatt*   *between things
And the mynd,
    Whiche leaves
Neither muchel-whatt*   *sundry things
2010   Nor mynd
Unnwharrfed.*   *unchanged

THOMAS:
Yes.
    One must thynk of
2015 Knouing-a-thing
    As an act of bountiffulnesse,
Or salvific compensacioun
    For the exclusivity and
Discreteness of things.[105]

2020 GOOBET:
And we have astahelede*   *settled
    That the Soul
Mediates al-thing.
    As Aristotle sayde,
2025 *"The Sawle* is*   *soul
    In a mannyr
    Al things."[106]

THOMAS:
Yes, That's right.
2030   Knowledge is a
Corrective or

Remedye
For the isolation
Of substauntive beings.[107]

2035   FOL. 36 R

GOOBET:
Could you give an exaumple?

THOMAS:
Yes, all right.
2040   If one were to know
A salix* tre   *willow
Pendaunt ouer the
Dew Pond, [*pointing yonder to Impyngton Dew Pond*]
Our knowing of it
2045 Would be as much
An event
In the lijfe of the form
"Tree,"
As the tre
2050   In its salisia-ness,*   *willowy-ness
And in its growing.[108]
Just as a
Newly discovered
Montayn*   *mountain
2055 Gladeres.*   *rejoices
It prefers to be sene
Than to be y-climben;
I believe one daye
Men and women
2060   Will be gidi* ynough   *giddy, silly
To i-climben montayns,
With raggish and daffed
Lingel and cabeling,*   *harnesses and straps
And other
2065 Kinds of liftes and knottinge.
You can see [*patting his rounde paunche with satisfactioun*]

That it would
  Nowght be *for me*.

GOOBET:
2070 Oh, I see.
  So, an idea of a tree
Or a montayn
  Is not in any way
A mere representatioun
2075   Or feining figment,
As it might
  One daye be seen?[109]
In-wis, I hear'd
  An arte lecturer
2080 At efening class
  In my vilage colege
Say that, for Cézanne,
  The montayne
Whych he hadde peinted
2085 Was the oryginal
  Montaine it-self.[110]

[MR NO-NONSENSE *re-enters the conversatioun, lookyng a lytle
swoty of brow*]

MR NO-NONSENSE:
What?
2090   Do you meyn to posen
That trewth
  Is not preven*   *tested, proven
By a speculative comparisoun
  With the thyng it-self?
2095 I am iscandlet* and appalled,   *disturbed in mind, or shocked
  And need more
Of that chese-slathered
  Cardboard papir stuffe![111]
And may I

2100   Venture to posen
       That if you deny that you are
         Copying or counterfeiting a bus,
       You will ytake a
        Dyfferent view
2105   If that bus
       Bumps into you!
       Epistemology, bulky friar;
        Epistemology!
       Even Ibn Sina kneue
2110   This sort of thyng.
       The oonly way to
        Deal with a sceptic
       Is to get him
        On the rack
2115   And torture him
       Until he admits that
       The rake is reall,
        And the afflictioun is reall,
       And oonly then
2120   You can stoppe,
       Saying,
        "Well, I'm sorry,
       Old chepmon,*   *chap-man
        But I suspose that,
2125   With your philosophie
       It could not
       Sothfulli* hurt you!"   *truly, really

    THOMAS:
    Our Dominican
2130   Middel-erth wysdouum is,
       On the contrarie,
        That a philosophie
       That must resort
        To the exaumple

2135   Of torture
       Is a philosophie
       Of torture,
       In-deyd, a *credo*
       Both tortyous and tortyouring—
2140   Syns* evil and pain are   *since
       But privacioun—
       And folwingly*   *afterwards, hereafter
       Dissimulable and gilous.*   *misleading and crafty
       Sed Contra,
2145   With regard to your
       More extreme
       Exaumple of death,
       The earthly me
       Wold not be able
2150   To verify this at all,
       Syns death is not
       Ani-wat,*   *anything
       Or a bicoming in lijfe,
       As anouther of your
2155   Cambridge sages
       Will one daye outtellen.*   *declare
       And for this reasoun,
       It cannot, I am afrayd,
       Put any person—
2160   *Qua* person,
       Who is brethinge and conscious—
       Out of their miserie.
       For they cannot beliven it
       To enjoy their being ded.
2165   Only the future
       Of the soul
       Is in questioun,
       And that involves
       Further imaginable torture,

2170   Or some remissioun,
         Or else again, a delite
             So unimaginably wundyrfulle
         That it will not even include
             Any sensation of relefe.
2175   But, once more,
             I commit *digressio.*
         To retourn to
             My main *responsio:*
         Stemmen stille.*   *tarry, stay still
2180   You cannot
         Bandy about
             This ydea of a
         "Thyng itself."
             Swich a thyng is
2185   Only "itself"
             In its being
         Confoormed
             In the intellecte
         Of the knower,
2190   In its being *ordered*
         To a beautiful ratio
             Or proportioun.
         Everything is relational
             As well as substancial.

2195   GOOBET:
         Yes, Thomas is right.
             The thingli-itself is
         Only it-self
             By being well-lykened
2200   To the knower,
             And by its form entering
         Into the mind
             Of the knouer.
         Truth is not "mesured"

2205   In any way,
        But sounds itself,
        Resounds,
        Or shines outwardes
        In beaute.[112]

2210   THOMAS:
        Let's just checkke
        What we have so far fownd:
        Trewth is not
        Epistemological,
2215   To use your barbarine word,
        Mr No-Nonsense.
        It is convertible
        With Being.
        It is a
2220   Mode of existence.
        And it is related to a
        Particular aspect of Being,
        Whiche, accordyng to our
        Modus cognoscendi,
2225   Is received as a kynd of
        Analogical or beautiful
        Assimilatioun
        Betwyx thyngs.

        MR NO-NONSENSE:
2230   Now, look here,
        If trewth is—
        How do you put it?—
        "Convertible with Being,"
        And is a manner of
2235   Assimilatioun
        Betwyx thyngs,
        It seems that trewth is
        Disappointingly fugitif,
        Or doun-slidinge,

2240   Like a kind of
          Intermediate slori*   *mud, slime, slurry
       Or sloppes.
          Wher exactly *is*
       This trewth of yourn?
2245   At leest
       My kynd of trewth
          Is one you can
       Really poynt to!

THOMAS:

2250   The place of trewth [*adopting mistical tone*]
          Is many-fold and jerarchical,*[113]   *of the angelic hierarchy
       And one fynds it soukyngly*   *gradually
          By means of
       An ascendyng schale,
2255   Vpward procedyng.
       One might bygynnen by sayinge
          That truth is
       A property of thyngs,
          That a thyng is trewe
2260   If it ful-fills it-self
          And holds it-self
       Samneward,*   *together
          Accordyng to its
       Character and goal,
2265   As in Augustine's adopcioun
       Of the Stoic "housekeeping"
          As the innere sense.
       Who wold spread
          Gall on their tost?
2270   Or wed their darlyng with a
          Ring made of tinne?[114]
       So, ilike-wise, one can saye,
          "This is truew rein"*   *rain
       If it is reining very gretli.[115]

2275   MR NO-NONSENSE:
        Aha!!! A sloppy
            Metaphorycal instaunce
        Of the word "truew."
            I have rumblyd you!

2280   THOMAS:
        No, no, no.
            It is an enterly
        Propere use,
            As it here refers
2285   To the moste
            Ideal Reine,
        Reyne wete,*   *wet
            Reyne iful-filling* its   *fulfilling
        Operaciouns of lijfe,
2290   *Realysing its "second act"*
        Of expressive relacioun—
            In wis,
        Fallyng from the sky—
            And its "third act"
2295   Of exstaticallie*   *ecstatically
            Reachinge others
        As its goal,
            Makyng them
        Soaking weet,
2300   Whiche you know
        All about—
            And perfetly complecshen
        Collective goals
            Endelongue,*   *alongside
2305   Fulfilling the naturall cicle
            Of waterr,
        And ensuring
            A good hervest.
        By these means,

2310 In exceeding it-self,
      Apparauntly accidentally
      (For-so-much as
      It might other-wyse
      Remeyn in its substaunce
2315 In the nebulose* firmament),   *vaporous
      It bicomes
      More it-self
      Super-substancially.

      GOOBET:
2320 Do you mene, Thomas,
      That a thyng is deemed
      "Less trewe"
      If it is distourbed
      Or impeded
2325 In some way
      From its
      Ordinary operaciouns,
      Whether by poisoun
      Or sickeling,
2330 Or some other droublinge?*[116]   *disturbance

      THOMAS:
      Exactly.

      GOOBET:
      So, we have asked,
2335 "Where is truth?"
      And your andwurden* was   *answer
      That trewth is
      In a thing
      When it is
2340 Ful-fylling its purpos,
      Its *telos*.

      But whatt is bifalling
      When a thyng is

Ful-filling its *telos*?
2345   How does it unto-come there,
And where exactly is "there"?
Is "there" a deu-plashe*   *dew pond
Or a hyrst,
Or the remote skyes,
2350   Or a cool-eied* far-awey sterre?   *eyed

THOMAS:
A thing is
Ful-filling its *telos*
When it is
2355   *Copying Godde*
In its own manere—
Godfullyche—*   *graciously
And tendyng to existence
As knowledge
2360   In the divyne Minde:
An oke tre copies Godd
By beyng trewe
To its tre-ness,
Reyn by being reiny,
2365   And the deu
Submytting to
Your plashe—and so and so.[117]

GOOBET:
This does not astoneiden* me.   *surprise
2370   In wis, I hadde
Al-ways assumed
That thyngs were so.

THOMAS:
Now, if a thyng
2375   Is mooste trewe
When it is
Purposly dyrecten,

And that means,
  When a thyng is
2380 Copying Godde,
  Then this wold suggest
That trewth is fountamentally
  In the Mynd of Godde
And oonly secundaryly
2385   In thyngs,
As copying
  The Mynd of Godd.

GOOBET:
Any suggestioun, therefor,
2390   That you have a
Realyst theory of trewth
  As a simple
Correspondence
  Of mynd to thyng
2395 Is here quyte
  Out of the questioun.

MR NO-NONSENSE:
[almooste aborst] As if it were not suffisaunt
  That truth is beauty, and beyng,
2400 And that the whole thyng
  Is dubiously
And speculatively
  Metaphisicalle,
And not epistemological!
2405   This really is
Too mucche.
  Lok here,
Accordyng to my
  Proper varyant
2410 Of correspondence theory,
  I can claim

An unmediated
A-conceptual
And more or less *intuitive*
2415   (Though I am waren*   *wary, vigilant
Of that word)
Apprehensioun of thyngs,
But nowe you tell me
That when one
2420   Knoues a thyng,
One does nought
Know that thing
As it is in itself,
But ferforthlie* as   *altogether
2425   One grasps it
As imitatyng Godde,
Godd that made
Al thyng of noght.

                                                      FOL. V 41

2430   GOOBET:
Please say mor,
Mr No-Nonsense.

MR NO-NONSENSE:
Well, one would *usuely*
2435   See imitatioun
As a secondari,
And folwingly
Less autentik*   *authentic
Operacioun of lijfe,
2440   Al-outly a bit
Dodgy,
Like plai-acting;[118]
Or like one of those
Handi-dandi* made-up podinge,   *underhand, involving bribery
2445   An umbegilded idiocy.
But here it semes

That imitatioun is
The highest forme
Of autentikiti* attaynable   *authenticity
2450   For materiall thyngs,
*As if the counterfeit plai**   *theatrical performance
Were the thyng it-self,
The trewe tragedie.[119]

THOMAS:

2455   I see no-thyng wronge with that.
The placyng of imitatioun
Ahead of autonomy
Suggests that
Borrowing is
2460   The overmooste verrynesse
Whych can be attained.[120]
There wyll be a tyme
When peple
Will *lose all wondringe,*
2465   By assumyng that they
Must alwey be
Originale,
And that copying is
But obsolescence.
2470   Rathur, one must copy
In order to be,
And one continues
In beying oonly as a copy—

GOOBET:

2475   And never
In one's own ryght.[121]

THOMAS:
So, when human-kende senses,
And the enllumyned intellect
2480   Receives into it-self

The species of the
Materiall substaunces
Whiche it knows,
It does not knoue them
2485   In the mannyr of
An *arreinement**   *arraigning, laying out for display
*Of unmoving** facts.*   *unmoving, static

Rather, the senses sense
Theyr *delight*
2490   *In the things,*
And the reasoun
Doubles delite
By mesuring or distinguen
Whather they are
2495   Truwe to theim-selves.[122]
That is, if they are
Whaght they seme to be,
And al is
Going accordyng to plan.
2500   Other-wyse, the senses
Will be squaimous,*   *nauseated, squeamish
And the jugement offendet.

GOOBET:
You mene that
2505   Even correspondyng
To finyte objects
Is correspondyng
As farre as possible
To the Mynde of Godd?

2510   THOMAS:
Yes, you inspirate bumpkin.
In the fyrst place,
The minde must judge whether,
For exaumple,

2515   A tree is beying
            Treue to it-self,
        Or the reyn reyning
            In a gretly drenchinge fashioun,
        Accordyng to the mynd's
2520   Divyne inner
        Light of yllumynatioun,
            Even on a sunne-less daye.
        By doing this,
            The mynd discerns
2525   An analogical proportioun
            Of thyngs to Godd,
        And fynds here
            A manifestatioun
        Of the invisibile
2530   In the visyble.
        In wis, the oonly thyng
            That distynguishes
        Mynde as mynde
            Is this discernment of
2535   The Mynde of Godd.
            Othyr-wis, it would iust be
        A power
            Able to beweld*   *dominate
        The senses
2540   And non-sceadwislic beestaile,*   *non-rational beasts
        By its capacity
            To distaunce it-self
        Through reflectioun
            And then
2545   To impose it-self
            As the will to dominate.
        Thus Augustine, in the treatise
            I have al-redy mentiouned,
        Says that whatt proues*   *proves

2550   Our human reasoun
       Is our power to tame
       And domesticate
       Anymals.[123]
          But he goes on to say that,
2555   If it were just
       A mattere of
       Species-ist dominacioun,
          We wold have bisunken
       Into a besteli*   *debased
2560   Anymality we-self.
       It is oonly bicause
          We gouerne beestaile wiseli,
       Under Godd,
          That we can be sayd
2565   To thynk at al.
          The same goes, he argues,
       For our governing of our
          Own boddies and senses.[124]

       GOOBET:
2570   [*in rapture*] Oh! So, whatt it fynds
          In nature,
       And whatt it orders
          Nature by,
       Is Beauty—
2575   Whiche "pleases" the sight,
       And delites the jugement.[125]
          I thynk I have alwais suspected
       Som-thyng like this,
          As on one of those
2580   Charminge niyhts
          Whiche gives more delite
       Than a hundred lukky dais,
          As the poete[126] seien.

MR NO-NONSENSE:

2585 I just do not
Understaund it.
Wistly knouledge demaunds
An homble submissioun
Of subjectivity
2590 Bifore the
Unmeving* objective?   *unmoving
Other-wise, it is
Some sough or seuer*   *marshy bog or drainage ditch
Kynd of knouledge!

2595 THOMAS:

No, no, no.
In knouewing som-thyng,
A sotil* proporcioun   *delicate
Bitwix the objective
2600 And the subjective arises.
If one requires
A beautiful apperaunce,*   *appearance
Whether glimpsed
Or brought about,
2605 In order to manifeste the trewth,
Then, while it is in-wis
The objective
That is regystered,
This can oonly be regystyred by the
2610 Subjectively in-formed power
Of rightly desyring
Sighte and jugement.

GOOBET:

So, we knowe,
2615 When we see an oke tre,
That is treue;
It is one whose
Tre-ness

Is gretly goode
2620   At imytating Godd.
This is not som-thyng
That we knowe
In a fact-lyke way,
But more as knouing
2625   A mannere of lijfe.
But in knoueing
The tre-ness
Of a tre,
Is that al
2630   We are knoueing?
Just imitatioun?

THOMAS:
Well, actually, no.
We are knouinge
2635   A gret deal more.
Syns the oke tre
Transmits tree-ness —
For sothly, oonly exists —
As imytating Godd,
2640   Whatt we receyve,
In trewth,
Is a participatioun
In the drihtness.*   *divine Godhead
To put this any-wother wey,
2645   In knewing an oke tre,
We are cacching it
On its way
Back to Godd,
Or, forsothly,
2650   We are entryng
Godd's perpetuall
Retorn to Him-self
Goddfullyche.*   *graciously

GOOBET:

2655   You do not mean to suggeste
     That this is a glidinge
    Or a bestiringe
     In the sense of
    A discursive passage
2660   From unknouen
    To knouen?

THOMAS:

No, it's an encercling,
   And mooste entanglings hath,
2665 A glidinge out
    From Him-self,
  And retourning
    To Him-self,
Alwais aredy
2670   Ful-wroght*   *completed
From the biginninge
    Of ay-wilday.*   *eternity
For Godd, in knoueing
    His own escence,
2675 Al-so knoues other thyngs
    In whichee he sees
A likeness of Him-self,
    Syns he grasps Him-self
As participable-in,
2680   And so He retourns
To His essence.[127]

FOL. 47 R

[MR NO-NONSENSE *sits down and puts his head in his hands*]

GOOBET:

2685 Poor Mr No-Nonsense.

THOMAS:

Look here, Mr No-Nonsense,

I thynk you hadde better
Blok your eres,
2690   Bicause if you hear
What I am about to say,
It might be
Your undoinge.
You see,
2695   As al-redy mentiouned,
I am quyte influenced by Aristotle
When I say that
Even the human soule
Is fundamentally
2700   An anymal soule,
Or a "form of forms"
Whiche holds together
A living materiall organism.
I see intellect as merely
2705   A power of the soule,
Rather than its essence.

GOOBET:
Goodness. You have friknesse.*   *courage

THOMAS:
2710   Too right I do.
The power of the mynde
Is in som-way
"Accidental" to us.[128]
What this means is that
2715   Som-thyng semi-accidental
Rises above its
Proper positioun,
And comes to dyfinisshe*   *define
A thyng's essence
2720   Biyond its essence,
In a super-essential way.

Hence, the human anymal
   Need not "thynk,"
Bicause that is just a
2725   Chaunce invocatioun
And communicatioun
   Of the dyvine power
To govern the world,
   But oonly when it does so
2730   Is it human—

GOOBET:
—and the more it exercyses
   Its power of intellect,
The more
2735   It is human![129]
Oh! [in rapture]

MR NO-NONSENSE:
Look here, I'm not lilie-livered!
   I can cope with all your
2740   Nifly* poppycock!   *raggish, silly
   To posen
That intellectioun
   Is a borrowed power
Verily adoun gan send*   *casts down
2745   The human mynde
So that it is a
   Certein kynd of dong-hep.*   *dung-heap

THOMAS:
No, no. Not a bit of it.
2750   May I draw your attentioun,
Mr No-Nonsense,
   To the Neoplatonic legacie of the
Metaphisics of participatioun?
   Our capacitie
2755 For thowght

Is by no means
A reuthfully
Humiliated endevour,
But is a partial receyving
2760   Of dyvine intellectioun
Whycch is at one
With the dyvyne regnance.
We oonly exist humanly,
Accordyeng to a
2765   Higher kynde of lijfe,[130]
Exercysing our intellect,
By participatyng in knoueledge
And sharing in a kynd of
Eternal politik.
2770   It semes that
What is extra to us
Most dyffinesshes* us.   *defines

GOOBET:
So, intellectioun is
2775   Akyn to grace,
Bicause the mooste importaunt part of us
Is not part of oure anymal essence at al,
But is super-added to us,
Properly and yet accidentalli.[131]

2780   MR NO-NONSENSE:
I would lik to go back
To the qwestioun of the
Difference betwyx
Godd's knoueledge
2785   And human knoueledge.
Yo have tryed to shewe that,
Despit appearaunces,
You do not make intellectioun
What you curyously calle

2790   An illusory
        Or humiliated enterpryse.
        But, it semes there is a
        Gret differens
        Betwix oure relatioun
2795   To knoueledge,
        And that of Godd,
        Who knowes by
        His very Essence?

THOMAS:
2800   Most fountamentally.
        Followyng Pseudo-Dionysius
        And Augustine,
        I have tried to move biyond
        Pagan Neoplatonists,
2805   For wham
        The One and the Good
        Lay biyond the
        Subjective and psychic,
        And ineffably
2810   Above *Nous*.
        I am keen to inbring
        A certayn nute*   *note
        Of relationality
        And differaunce
2815   Into our notion of God,
        Even bifore dilatyng
        An holy Thrillihodie Theologie.*   *Trinitarian theology

GOOBET:
        Is that why you mentioun
2820   Godd's knoueledge
        Of the modes
        In whych He can be participated?

THOMAS:

Yes. In this way,

2825   Godde knows the creacioun.

He knoues thyngs fully

  In knouing their ends,

Their perfectioun,

  Whiche includes

2830   All that they are.

GOOBET:

That is very comfortinge,

  I can tell you!

THOMAS:

2835   I'll tell you som-thyng els besydes.

  It is this differaunce

Betwix Godd's

  Manner of knoueing

And oure owne,

2840   Whiche maks

Oure manner of comprehencioun,

  In a straunge and entirly

Humble way,

  Godd-lyke.

2845 GOOBET:

I knewe it all along.

THOMAS:

That does not stonnede* me.   *surprise, stun

  God, as cause of knoueing,

2850   Is in Him-seilf

  Plentifully knoueing,

And is not simply

  An inscrutable

And unconne*   *unknown

2855   Cause of our knoweledge.

For this reasoun,
  We can know som-thyng—
Ani-wat,*   *anything
  Albeyt remotely—
2860 Of Godd's
  Knoweing of Him-self.

GOOBET:
Is that the same
  As when you say
2865 We can analogically predicate
  Knoueledge of Godde?

THOMAS:
Yes!
  Al-though our owne
2870 Imitatiouns
  Of Godd's knoweledge
Are marked by
  Imperfectioun
And diuersite;
2875   Yet even here,
What seems a deficience
  In our *modus*
Bitoknens its
  Own remedie,
2880 And is a kynd of
  Perfectioun.[132]

GOOBET:
That comes as
  Good news
2885 For bumpkins.

THOMAS:
Yes, I can ymaginen.

MR NO-NONSENSE:
Wait a minut.
2890   Wistly Godd's
Ful-thriven knoueledge
Of Hym-self
Wold be
In no way divers?
2895   Wisly it must be
Absolute oneness,
As for the
Neoplatonic traditioun,
If that is what we have
2900   To talk abowt?
Only One
Can outwandre
From the One.

THOMAS:
2905   Yes, Mr No-Nonsense,
But Godd's One-ness
Contayns withinne it-self
Superabundaunt pleynitude
Whiche our diversitie —
2910   Or very difference from Godd —
Seeks to express,
Albeyt analogically.

[MR NO-NONSENSE *underspekyng obscenities under his breth*] ¹³³

GOOBET:
2915   Oh, this is all
Moste satisfactorie.
I lyke the ydea
That there is
A way in whych
2920   Oure kynd of knoueledge
Echoes God's way
Of knoueing thyngs.

ACT TWO
SCENE 2

[MR NO-NONSENSE *tries to get the uppere hand*]

MR NO-NONSENSE:

2925 .....Aha! [*sounding a bit smug*]
But ther stille remayns
The thorny questioun
Of *Godd's knoueledge*
Of singulars;
2930   This, wistly,
Radicaly differenes
Our manner of knowing
From that of Godd.¹³⁴
For al-though Godd is
2935 Pure Mynd,
Withuten remaynder,
And there-for
A more spyrituall
Kynd of knouer
2940 Than human beyngs,
Never-lesse,
His knoueledge is more
Substancial
Than oures,
2945 Ferforthly as He al-one
Fully knows singlers,*   *individuals, singulars
And the principles
Of their individuatioun,
Whiche to us must remayne
2950 Some-wat cloudious.
That is the kynd of thyng
You mediaevale types thynk,
And the kinde of ydiom

In whych you lyke
2955   To put thyngs.[135]

THOMAS:
Very goode questioun,
    Thowgh I have to adde
That if I am in-wis
2960   *Per typus*
Of the Middle era
    Of Middle-erth,
This is bicause
    I am in fact a reell
2965   Mediaeval god-man,
        As *you* wold put it.
In-wis, when we
    Knoue a thiyng,
We cannot
2970   Directly apprehende
Its materiall individuatioun,
    Syns, followyng Aristotle,
Matter cannot inwend
    The human intellect,
2975   Any more than it can
        Cause matter to exist.
Actually, Goobet,
    You'll be pleased to hear
What I am about to say.
2980   You see,
As I mentioun
    In my *Disputatiouns*,
Godd is more of a
    Country bumpkin,[136]
2985   Capax of conyng* by a   *capable of understanding
    Brut dyrect intuitioun
Of cluddish erth,
    Than a lerned scholar.

GOOBET:

2990 Lesse of the
Brut and cluddish,
If you don't mynd!

THOMAS:

Sorry. But Godd's mynde,
2995 Al-thogh immateriall, is
(In a misterial way)
Commensurate with matter,
Syns Godd
Creaytes matter.

3000 GOOBET:
—Bicause Godd
Maks matter,
So he kens it?

THOMAS:

3005 Yes. But this does not mene
That He receives
Matter into Him-self;
He does not receive forms
Or speycies either.
3010 Rather, He knoues
By His very essence,
And knoues thyngs
Outwith Him-self
Enterly by His
3015 Plentivous productivitie—
Form and matter a-lyke—
For both are
Fountamentally
Thyngs in existaunce.

3020 GOOBET:
My goodnesse;

At this poynt,
You have moved
A longe way away
3025   From Aristotle!

THOMAS:
Alas, hou-ever,
Mr No-Nonsense,
I cannot, for al that,
3030   Aspire to the
Noble estate of
Bumpkinhood,
Where singlers
Can be espyed
3035   In all their
Singularity.[137]

GOOBET:
Whoppe wow!

THOMAS:
3040   Or can we?
It semes that a
Bitoken bumpkinhood
May accrue to us.
Biyond Aristotle,
3045   I have recently developed
An accownt
Of how we do,
In a certayn meaure,
Participate in
3050   The dyvine knoueledge
Of singlars.
Godd, as we have seen,
Knoues singlars in tyme
Bicause He is
3055   Tyme-lessly

Outwith theym,
  And bryngs theim to be
From no-thyng.
  Hou-ever, by emphasising
3060 The nature of
  Human knouledge
As an event,
  An unstintinge mouement,
And a dynamic interactioun
3065   Betwix soule and body,
We detect
  A certayn remote
Adequatioun
  Or approximatioun
3070 To the dyvyne
  Manner of knouing.
You see, biyond Aristotle,
  I have dilated
An account of knowledge
3075   As a relaye system
Of significatioun,
  Or conveyaunce,
As if the aiyr
  Were a bruschet-thicket*   *a thicket of bushes
3080 Of invisible cheynes,*   *chains
  Heng-puliues* and scaffotts.*[138]   *suspended pulleys * scaffolds

                                                    FOL. 46 V

[MR NO-NONSENSE *gladdens at the mentioun of chaiens and
heng-pulleys;* GOOBET *looks a little glum*]

MR NO-NONSENSE:
3085 Please could you explayn this
  More clerly?
I like the sound of
  An identifiable
Mechanism at last.

3090   THOMAS:
        Yes, of course.
            Let us consult
        This useful mappe [*points to fygure 1*]
            Whiche shows the journeye undertaken
3095   In knowing a truncheoun, or cricket bat—

        GOOBET:
        —a singular, if ever there was one!
            But how forsothly
        Does a Neapolitan
3100   Come to knoue
        The gamen of cricket?

        THOMAS:
        Never mynd . . .
            Our yse-creem* purveiours   *ice cream
3105   Are al-way in search of
            New retayl outlets.
        In any case, this journeye involves taking
            Thre different trayn carts.

        GOOBET:
3110   Your merchaunts
            Cannyt have told you aright . . .
        Cricket is
            A rusticalle recreacioun
        With no need of
3115   Tounisshe* devyces;   *of the town, urban
        No-thyng but solid salix
            And well-tauni* lether.   *tanned

        THOMAS:
        Like any degonys,*   *bumpkin, or yokel
3120   You are easily diuerted
        By an ymage,
            And lose sighte of

What the ymage conveis.
I am comparing knoueledge
3125 Of any-wat thyng
To a train journei,
Chauncefulliche*   *perhaps
On your to-bee-famows
Lunden Vndergrounde?
3130 Per-happes on your waye
To see a Cricket "test matcch"
At the famows Lorde's grund?

GOOBET:
I like not the soun of
3135 This newe ymage.
Cricket, yes,
But we do not hold hereabouts
With no Lundon doctryn . . .

Fygure 1: Underground Train ("Tube") map of understanding, based on Aquinas'
De Veritate, Q1–4

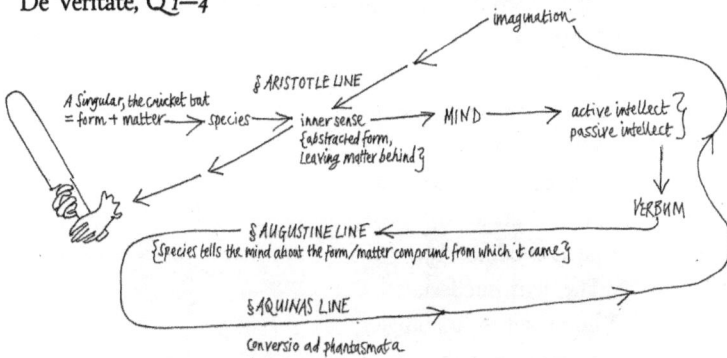

THOMAS:
3140 Prithee sylence!
Trayn Journey No. 1 is on
The Aristotle Lyne.
Here, the forme leaves
The statioun of

3145   Individual substaunce,
         The hylomorphic
            Form/matter compound,
         And enters into
            The Siphon
3150   Or Tubbe of Abstractioun.
            As it journeis further
         Into the tunnel,
            The form bicomes "species,"
         And is further abstracted
3155   As it passes
         Through the "senses"
            Of the mannish biholdere,*   *human observer
         Then into
            The Doubling of sense,
3160   Whych is the inner sense,
            And then into the
         Phantasmicall
            And spectral imaginatioun
         Of this sensatioun,
3165   Finally to arrive at the ultymate
         Aristotelian destinatioun
            Of the Mynde.
         Here, the ymagyned ymage
            Arrives at,
3170   And is modified by,
            The actif intellect,
         Yllumyned in knouinge,
            To produce a species,
         Whiche the passive intellect
3175   Then receives.

         Necst, there is a
            Chaunge of platforme
         Onto a dyfferente, faster,
            More self-propelled trayn.

3180   The known species
            Is articulated or expressed
        By the *Verbum* or inner worde,
            As Augustine announced to us.[139]

GOOBET:
3185   Where can this be taking us? [*Still looking puzzled*]

THOMAS:
        Well, *Trayn Journey No. 2* is on
            The Augustine Lyne.
        Here, biyond Aristotle,
3190   I propose that a concepte
        Does not just
            Leave matter bihind.

GOOBET:
        Tarrye, tarrye.
3195   What did Aristotle thynk?

THOMAS:
        For Aristotle,
            The materiall element
        Was seen as
3200   Inymycal to understaunding—
        It was related to
            Irrational formless cahos.
        But for Augustyne,
            Matter is creayted by Godd,
3205   And ther-fore
            Proceeyds from myind.
        So, if our mynd,
            In order to understaund,
        Must abstract from matter,
3210   This is for Christian
        And Jewish and Islamic follc,
            A deficiency of understaynding.

MR NO-NONSENSE:

3215 So, you are wronge, thane?

THOMAS:

Anbididen,* dear fellawe.   *hold on
   The purpys of *Journey No. 2* is
To compensayte som-wat
3220   For this deficience,
Bicause here,
   The nocioun,
As inner worde,
   Is liyke a signe—

3225 GOOBET:

Do you mene,
   Like a signacle*   *sign
In so muchel as it
   Poynts awey from it-self
3230 By means of its ne-the-les
   Essential and behoving mediacioun,
Back to whatt it represents?

THOMAS:

Exactly. As Augustyne sees it;
3235   All knouledge
Is intentional,
   As retournyng
To concret thynges
   Whiyh we cannot fully vnderstonde.

3240 GOOBET:

Mmmmm.
   This concours wyth the
Foisoun* of intellect   *abundance
   As intentioun
3245 With desir,

Whiche retourns us to thyngs,
Encourageng us to
    Ylearern more of them,
Sithen to *entend* sum-thyng
3250   Is to *desire* to knoue more
Of the truwth of the thyng—
    This gol beyng regarded
As a goode.[140]

THOMAS:
3255   Yes. In wis, I lyke to thinke
    That I have
    A clearer sense
    Than Aristotle
    Of knoueledge
3260   As a never ful-wroght projecte,
    A lif-werk of loue.*[141]   *love

Trayn Journey No. 3
    Is on my very owne
Franchysed leine
3265   Whych taks us back
To wher we bigan,
    But allowes us to see
Our poynt of departire
    Very differently.
3270   The Augustyne Leiyne, you see,
    Stil does not help us to explayne
How we have any
    Glimeringe of singlars.*   *glimmering or inkling of singulars

MR NO-NONSENSE: [*smugly*]
3275   No, in wis it does not.
    But I do not quyte gette
All this goyng rounde
    In cercles vndergrunde.
It could all get very costable, you knoue—

3280   And all for wat?
        We will neuer unto-come
            At Lorde's this wai,
        Let al-one
            Be in tyme for
3285   The openinge tosse.

        THOMAS:
        Pacience!
            As I fore-sayde,
        Hou-ever much the signacle
3290   Poynts us back
        To the form/mattere composit,
            We stille cannot be certayn
        That it exists,
            Syns mattere cannot
3295   Enter into the mynde.
            Here, I dilate—
        And I lyke to thinkke this is
            Rathere originale—
        A theory of the imaginatioun—

3300   GOOBET:
        Oh, long bifore Kant or Coleridge!

        THOMAS:
        Yes, but actuellie,
            Followyng sum indicatiouns
3305   In the *Liber de Causis*,
            And certayn asydes in Augustyn,
        I thynk that
            Whanne-ever we *sense*,
        We al-so *imagine* sum-thyng,
3310   Bicause imaginatioun
        Is the misterial
            Poynt of fusioun
        Betwix inner sense and intellect.

Sensing *that* we are sensing
3315 Leads naturally
To a fantasysed *repetitioun*
Of this sensing,
And this turne-by-turne
Brings us neighlen
3320 To the abstract
"Distaunce" of intellect.
We tend not to be aware of this,
But actuallye,
We have to imagen
3325 Even the thyngs that we
Realy do see,
If we are to have
Any ydea of them.

MR NO-NONSENSE:
3330 I'm feeling a bit wit-losen . . .
In trewth.

ACT THREE
SCENE 1

[THOMAS, GOOBET *and* MR NO-NONSENSE *sittinge vnder a tre*]

THOMAS:
Let us bilokenn backwardes.
3335   We have seen that
The acte of intellectioun
    Is accidentale to us,
And yet difynes our nature
    As human beyngs.
3340 And this has led us
    To enserch
The possibilite
    That oure nayture
As human beyngs
3345   Is paradoxically,
By definitioun,
    To exceed our nature,
And to enjoy forder
    "Accidental" participatiouns
3350 In the diviyne.
    We have seen,
Fordor-over,
    That this semes to be
The case
3355   In severell ways,
But pryncypaly
    In the excercyse
Of oure imaginatioun—

GOOBET:
3360 —But how does
    This helpe us

To knoue
Materiall singlars?

THOMAS:
3365 —Bicause not oonly do we
Passe throwgh
The imaginatioun,
On the way
To knoueledge,
3370 But al-so
We go backe
To the imaginatioun
In order to complet
Our acte of vnderstaundyng.
3375 I call this third journei,
On my own Leine,
"The Retourne to the phantasm."
For al thogh the intellecte
Cannot *on its owne*
3380 Knoue singlars,
It can after all
Reacch them
With the aid of the
Phantasising power...

3385 [*Thondringe and lightenyng*]

THOMAS:
You have terryble wederinge!*   *weather
And ther may be
Further paryties too
3390 Betwix the way
Godd knoues
And the waye
We knoue.

GOOBET:
3395 For exaumple?

THOMAS:
Well, ytake the way thaht
  Human knoueledge
Has a self-expressif
3400   Or creatif dimensioun
In its need for the use
  Of outwardinge werds—

GOOBET:
Yes, you have mentiouned
3405   The "aesthetic" momente
Wher-thurgh one must judge
  The beauty
Of a particuler proportioun.

THOMAS:
3410   And there is al-so the aspect
  Of imitatioun or *mimesis*—

GOOBET:
—And the excercyse
  Of imaginatioun,
3415   Whicch you thynk of
  Not as a
Passif receptacle,
  Nor inert and unmeving facultie,
But as a
3420   Gatheryng up
Of ymages
  Whiche modifies them
In a creative way—

THOMAS:
3425   Yes. And one
  Should not foryet
The dynamic movement, or
  Displacement of energy
Envoluped in knoueledge—

3430 MR NO-NONSENSE:
—Whycch is
  Wholly vn-like
My own
  More modern
3435 Nocioun of
  Knoueledge
As an unmeving onluken
  Or mirroring.

THOMAS:
3440 In-wis, and here
  One could mentioun
The way in whiche Plato
  And Neoplatonic traditioun,
More radically
3445 Than Aristotle,
Were prepared to see
  Knoueledge
As a kynde of
  Transiting motioun,
3450 A kinetic acctioun,
  Like weaving,
And I am willinge
  Cautiously to concurre.

[*more thondringe, and distant cloppineg of horse hooves*]

3455 In-wis, I can thynke of
  Severall exaumples
Of a reall processioun
  In the mynde:
Conclusiouns
3460 *Really proceede*
From principlys;
  An actuall conceptioun
Really proceedes

From habitual knouledge;
3465   Our ydeas
        Abowt the essences
Of subordinate thyngs
        Proceede from ydeas
About the essences
3470   Of higher thyngs.[142]

GOOBET:
Euen when the mynde
        Vnderstonds yt-self,
It thynks of
3475   An expressioun,
And not dyrectly
        Or reflexively
Of the mynde.

THOMAS:
3480   Yes. Whan the mynde
        Vnderstonds yt-self,
It must proceede
        From it-self,
Or express it-self,
3485   Juste as the werd
In the intellecte is
        Expressed by an agent
Distingt from yt-self.

This emanative expressioun,
3490   In contraste to Aristotle,
For whom *energeia* was
        Discrete,
Transitively proceedes,
        As sublymated *kinesis*,[143]
3495   And in som ways
        Can be seene as *crafte-lyke*,
As a constructioun or internall

Operatioun of arte,
In-so-muchel as the processioun
3500   Of the worde involves an
Vnfoldyng of thowght
Whych is,
By a corious paradox,
Oryginally constitutive of it.
3505   In sucche a way that
There is no oryginal thowght
Withuten swich an
Expressive dilatioun,
And no orygin
3510   Withouten a repetitioun.[144]

FOL. L R

GOOBET:
Is that why the fynall
And efficiente cause—
3515   Both ende and archetype—
Of externall expressiouns,
As descrybed in *De Veritate*
As the *verbum cordis*,
Should be seene
3520   Not as an unmeving ideall,
But as akyn to the
Interior shaping forme
Of *ars*
Involved in al exterior
3525   Artistic expressioun?

THOMAS:
Exactly so, my goode *rusticus*.
Suche an *ars* or *verbum*
Must yt-self
3530   Come into beyng,
By a kinde of anterior
Creative *supplementatioun*—

JACQUES:
[*from a great height,*[145] *interpolates*] Ah Oui!

3535 THOMAS:
Did you hear som-thyng...?
  Ani-wei, this suggests thaht
Al human knoueing
  Ys to be seen
3540 As an artistic productioun,
  Whych agayn emphasyses
That trewth
  Is an ontologicall mattere,
And not epistemologicall,
3545   Synce it is
In this way construed
  As an event
Rather than
  As a mirrouring.[146]

3550 GOOBET:
But how can we be sure
  Of any of this?
Our certeynty is in
  Concret thyngs,
3555 But howe do we knoue
  That Godd can
Stoope down to them?
  Wold He not actually
Have to vnto-come...

ACT THREE
SCENE 2

3560 *[Enter ffour passinge dronken trybesmen from The Trybe of Naturalistes, retournyng secrete-wyse from The Triangle Clubbe, disguyzedly apareiled in* FOX, RAT, WEASEL *and* STOAT *(respectively) tails and corresponding ffurre earres.*[147] *Unobserved by those on The Grene.]*[148]

STOAT:
I must say, thate was
   A pleasaunt colloquie
And a good repaste,
3565   Aspecially the puddyng![149]
But I am
   More and more
Outragyn to ileorn
   That ther are
3570 Other trybes
   Who iwish to
Denyte realte,
   Everi-thyng we all
Knoue to be trewe!
3575   We all *knoue*
There is one
   Byg fact
Whych we are all
   Snarleyned in,
3580 Like a puddyng,
   But we us-self,
The courrans,*   *currants
   As it were,
Are just self-enterclosed
3585   Buffered bopples,*   *bubbles
Seeing whan-so-ever

We want to see
In our swevenes,*   *dreams
Thowgh thagt has
3590   No-thing to do
With the trewth.
But now I hear
That there are
Other peple
3595   Livinge on the
Other side of
The unpassible
Firy equator,
In som-thyng called
3600   "The global sowth,"
Who thynk
Juste the opposit!
Realte is one byg
Phantasie bopple
3605   In whych we
Al commoune,
But the physicall wurlde
Is diuers,*   *diverse
Ful of fikelnesse
3610   And unstedfastnesse.
But mucch more
Monstruousli,
It has com to my ears [strokede furry stoat ears]
That in Cam-bridge yt-self,
3615   There is a new school of
Gidy mock-Thomists
Who enclaim thaht
Everi-wat-thyng
Ever-wat-wher
3620   Is al
Myxyd—*   *mixed together

Puddyng and courrans,
  Solidd and frothe.
It mooste be the influens of
3625   Lurkinge
Fenlond trybes-men
  And ther
Incorrigibyll totemism
  Abowt Pigges,
3630 Eles and Blak-birdes.[150]

FOX:
I too have herde
  These troublyng remours —
Christiens outspreding
3635 *Lesses* abowt Aquinas*,   *lies, untruths
Whom we knowue
  To have been
Alles wrong,
  But very resouninge,   *rationally sound
3640 And analytic,
  And so
Al-though misfening,*   *false
  Yet enterly precise,
And so, in a way,
3645 An absolutely
Iryght* atheist,   *correct
  As all sownd
Resoun-men like us are,
  Euen the relygyous ones.

3650 WEASEL:
I have cycled past
  Som of these loth-folk*   *despised people
On my way to the
  Biblet* refectory.   *library
3655 Charmyng but silly,

And unsuorprisingly
Som-tymes femele,
　Thoygh I cannowt rememor
The reasoun why
3660　　Ther ar womyn.¹⁵¹
One cold laughen
　If one were not so
Grichgidelich angry!
　Other trybe non-sense
3665　Abowt stones beyng treue,
　　Thyngs fleying
Back to theim-selves
　Through our thoughtes,
Aiery beyngs
3670　　Lynking euery-thyng
Up by the Goode! —
　*Vunderstille!**   *stop speaking!
Lest I be carried awey
　By this allectuous*   *seductive
3675　Jogeleri* non-sense me-self!   *entertainment, jesting

STOAT:
But I am
　A bit confusid,
Weasel.
3680　　Does not our trybe belieue
That the stone *is* a
　Trewe parte
Of the one byg
　Sticky gleimi* puddyng?   *slimy, viscous
3685　I mean, is not
　Everi-thyng els
Just a vicious abstractioun?
　And I mean *vicious*!
These floaty thyngs
3690　　Can realich

Thorugh-stang* you knoue!   *[thoroughly] sting
They may look begiling,
But they are
Seriously nasti!
3695   Not that they are *reall*,
Of course,
But unreallich reallich
Very, very daungerous
All the sayme;
3700   Just as lyable
To for-biten* as the   *bite
Nocioun* "dogge,"   *notion, idea
Whych of course
Tells me
3705   Absolutely no-thyng
About reall sikerli* hundes,*   *safe, certain *dogs, hounds
Whiche never forbite* at al,   *bite
And are al
Utterly singlar
3710   And incomparably
Differaunt
From one an-oother.
Even Gilliaum of Occam
Did not go
3715   Far enowgh
For my tastes.
Just not
Nomynalist enowgh!

FOX:
3720   Hold on, Clop-Stert,*   *Stoat
Old chapp!
Do not get so angre
That you sound lyke
One of those
3725   Frankish trybes-men

Who have it seymes
  Deconstrycted theim-selves,
Wat-so-ever thaht means,
  And of course
3730   It can nowt mean
  Ani-wat!

WEASEL:
Spekyng of whom:
  A sutil fot-note of
3735   *Wacche-word.**   *word of caution
  Some of the
Neue fenlond non-sense
  Does deryve from the
Frankish trybes-men, you knoue—
3740   Scandalouse
Non-cronical* stuffe   *not of the chronicles
  Abowt when
The modern
  Nocioun of metaphysik
3745   Was inuentyd,*   *invented
  As if it were not juste as
Primordiall or ancient
  As our trybe,
And its firrst elderlyng!*   *ancestor
3750   But, on the oother hand,
Some of these
  Galliene* druids,   *Of Gaul, Gallic
Thowgh they do have
  Madd ydeas,
3755   And do not wear
  Bicycle clipclapps,
Are ne-th-less
  Chapps lyke us!
They are *oure* sorte
3760   Of chappes,

Even thowgh Frankish,
And quyte
Weiward,*   *inclined to go counter to what is correct
If you knoue whatt
3765 I mean;
Sownd scholars,
In their owne wai,
Evun thowgh totally
Sotten* and blind-fellen*   *confused *misguided, as if blind-folded
3770 By a lot of
Daffed* stuffe;   *silly
But then they're
Frankish!
Al-wei,
3775 The long and
The shorte of it
Is that it wold be
Salubre*   *salutary
Not to assail
3780 *Them* directli,
But juste the
Fen-lond loth-folk
Who have no exscuse,
Beyng Englissh swayns,
3785 Whiche is succh
An embarrassment...

STOAT:
You twon are janglyng me!
I have not fynysht.*   *finished
3790 What really
Outrayges me
Is that these
Brutall fen-londers
Do not seem
3795 To knoue that

One can oonly vnder-stond
  Duns Scotus
If one redes him
  As a nominalyst,
3800 Bicause he was nowt one;
  And thenn
One wil see how
  Viciously treue
His doctryn
3805 Of the puddyng
As vnyuersally-
  Mereli*-eminesse-   *solely
But-throwgh-and-throwgh-
  In-all-its-varyed-
3810 Realte-*   *reality
  Truli-so-hard-core-as-
Scarceli-to-be-biteable,
  Really is.
And once one has
3815 Seen this,
Naturally one wyl
  Al-so see that
Thomas thowght
  Juste the same thyng!
3820 Univocity will save
  The harde-core
Safe bitts
  Of his teachyng,
In honest and sekyrly kepynge,*   *safe keeping
3825 Whiyh he expressed in
Juste one or two
  Pithee sowndbytes,
And then one will be able
  To see that,
3830 Of corse,

He really meynt* to   *intended, meant
Slingen all the reste
   Abowt analogi,
Participatioun,
3835   Luminous order,
Aungelic gouernment,
   Divyne pre-eminence,
Convenientia &c, &c.   *beautiful alignment

RAT:

3840 But hold on, old chap-stoat,
   I thowght you agreed that
None of thaht
   Was really
In Thomas at all,
3845   As I'm sure Weasel
Wold seccond.

WEASEL:

Yes in-wisa; [*nodding, and re-arraunging tail*]
   No trewth in the stones —
3850 Or more likely the mudd —
   For Thomas,
As the fen-londers
   So ludicrously claim;
And this may answer
3855   Your erer* concern, Stoat;   *earlier
Stones juste weiting*   *waiting
   To be knouen,
If perchaunce
   They are knouen,
3860 And thenn the trewth is juste
   In the bopples,
Excepte that *al* that
   The bopples
Are thynking,

3865   When they are not having
         Daffed phantasyes,*   *silly fantasies
            Is that
         The stone is truew—
            That is
3870   *Er um,*
            I mean—
         The stone
            Is a stone
         Is a stone,
3875   And thaht's al
         Ther is to it.

         STOAT:
         Well sayde, Weasel!
            All the saime,
3880   You have got to
            I-cnoulechie* thaht the   *acknowledge
         Aungelic Doctor
            Could some-tymes sound
         As if he hadde steped
3885   A byt outwith
         Our trybal line,
            And gowne* wher   *gone
         Oure peple
            Rightly
3890   Fearr to tredd,
            And evun hooly aungels
         Shold not,
            If they were reall,
         Whych they are not,
3895   Of corse.
         He really needed that
            Sutil* Scot   *perspicacious
         To shew hym,
            In an enginous* way,   *ingenious

3900   What he really meant
            Al-a-long,
        Whych was nothyng daffed,
            Or of yt-self sutil
        And aungelic at al.
3905   It was, of course,
        Juste *oure* puddyng,
            Whych we can see,
        Thurgh the
            Lumynous wallure*   *walls
3910   Of our courrans,
            Wallures whiche the
        Courrans-bopples
            Theim-selves diffine,*   *define
        Naturalli,
3915   And no-thyng els!
        No-thyng to do with
            An-wat*   *anything
        Outwith the wallure,   *outside the walls
            Syns Godd,
3920   With His treue
            Disynterest,
        Has fully given us
            To be
        Of ourselves,
3925   In juste the way that
        He is Hymselfe,
            The deare old chapp,
        Or wold be,
            If He weren't simply
3930   Part of a
            Distractyng gamen
        That I get payd
            A lot
        To plai.[152]

3935   Fortunateli,
        Even the chapps
          Who claymed once
        To play the gomen
          For reall
3940   Already knewue thaht,
          Even if there were
        A Godde,
          A byt lyke a
        Pryme courran
3945   Or raisin
        Sittyng on the topp
          Of the puddyng,
        He was stil stuck
          In the same
3950   Puddyng
          As the rest of us.
        By the wai,
          Al that was
        As mistical
3955   As you wyll get from me...
        We're not at all
          A mistical trybe,
        Are we?...

                              [*Exeunt into the eueningue mist-hakel*]
3960   [*roare of thonder*][153]

ACT THREE
SCENE 3

[Enter DEUS *equitando.* THOMAS *and* GOOBET *falle to their kne;* MR NO-NONSENSE *shuffles abowt a bit awkwardli, then falls to kne.]*

MR NO-NONSENSE:
Mmm...ah, yis! *[heilinge* DEUS]
   Wold you like
3965   A glass of sherry?
   I thunk we shold
Calle for the vicar!

DEUS:
My dear fellowes,
3970   I have been ryvettyd
By your emparlement.
   May I be so bolde as
To add a fot-note
   To wat you have
3975   Been sayinge?
   This paradigm
Of knouledge
   As co-originally
Self-expressif,
3980   Immediately poynts to
Me-self,
   As the thrilli-hod,*   *Trinity
Thereby suggestyng
   A certayn
3985   "Naturall" intimatioun
   Of this realte
In Me-self,
   Dispyte Thomas' explycit
Confynement

3990   Of the Thrillity
         To reveyled trewth.
             This occurs in two wais:
         Firrst,
             In the obvious sense
3995   Of bigetynge a word
             In and thurgh
         Its owne
             Essential realysatioun;
         And, secundly,
4000   In terms of the
         Manner of emanatioun
             Involved.
         This should be conceiyved
             In terms of the
4005   Ierarch of emanatiouns,
             Whych, Thomas,
         You ably descrybe
             In *Summa Contra Gentiles*,
         Where the higher the levele
4010   Of emanatioun,
         The more the processioun
             Or productioun
         Is in-wardly contayned,
             In succh a wey that I,
4015   As the mooste parfit beyng,
             Can emanate
         From Mi-self
             Withuten leavynge
         Mi-self,
4020   And retourne parfitly
         To Mi-self,
             Juste bi-cause I have
         Neuer dipartyd Me-self
             At al,

4025 Even thowgh
          I am alle leavyng,
       Syns my nature is
          Onlye of Love
       And Exstasie,
4030   Al out-goinge
       And procedyng fforyh,*   *forth
          And nought ellis,
       As the pagan sage
          Doth say,
4035   And my Good doctor
          Thomas recordys,
       I supremely retourn
          To My own essence,
       And thereby
4040   Wel wist* Mi-self   *know
       Pre-emynently.¹⁵⁴
          Sucche a contaynment
       Of emanatioun,
          One might thinke,
4045   Would be reseruyd for
          Me Al-one:
       God Fader and Sone and Holigost,
          God the Thrillihod,
       And threo persones in on-hod
4050   Withouten ende and biginninge.
       And yet it semes
          That Thomas'
       Laudatif ydea
          Of the in-ward word
4055   In the human intellect
          In a certayn way
       Remotely approximates
          In its manner of
       Comyng-forth

4060   To the in-wardly emanatyng
          Processioun within Me,
             The Godhede.
          For the human mynde
             Can produce a word
4065   That is distingt
             From iy-self,
          And yet remayns
             Withinne yt-self.
          The mynd is not relynxed*   *exhausted, fatigued
4070   Or up-spent
          By these nociouns
             (The innere words),
          And yet cannot be mynd
             Without its nociouns.

4075   MR NO-NONSENSE:
          Excuse me
             For interrupting You,
          Your Divyne Magesty.
             But what all this suggestes
4080   Is that correspondence,
             For Thomas'
          Theory of knoueledge,
             Means som-thyng
          More nuanced
4085   Than a mere mirrouryng
          Of realite in thowght.
             I thynk I starte
          To vnderstond thynges
             More playn nowe.
4090   There is an yntrynsyc
             Proportio or analogye
          Betwyx the mynd's
             Dryve towardes trewth,
          And the way thyngs

4095   Manyfeste them-selves,
     Whiche is theiyr
       Mode of beyng truew.
     This *proportio* is
       Experienced and assumed,
4100   But cannot be observed or
       Empirically confyrmed.
     It is assumed,
       Bi-cause mynd and thyngs
     Are both i-sheun*   *shown
4105   As procedyng
     From the dyvine creatif mynd,
       In swich a way that the
     Very sourse of thynges
       Is dymly ecco-ed
4110   In our mynds
       Whych generayte
     Vnderstonding.[155]

                                        FOL. LV V

DEUS:

4115   Yet it is al-so experienced,
     Bicause the concorde bitwix
     Mynd and thyngs,
       Ordayned by Me,
     The Godhede,
4120   Is not a nawghty*   *immoral, naughty
     Leibnizian pre-establishment
       Where no reall relatioun
     Bitwix mynd and thyngs,
       Taken as window-lesse moonads,
4125   Pertayns.
     Rather, the proportioun,
     Creatively ordered by Me,
       Betwix mynd and thynges,
     Really and dynamically flowend

4130   Bitwix them,
        And by receyving
          This proportioun,
        And actualisyng it,
          You human beyngs
4135   Come to knoue.

        MR NO-NONSENSE:
        Please do go on,
          Your Divine Majeste.

        DEUS:
4140   I don't mind if I do.
          If there can be corespondence
        Of thought to beings,
          This is oonly because,
        More fundamentally,
4145   Both beings and minds
        Corespond to
          My dyvyne *esse* and *mens*,*   *being and mind
        Or intellect.
          Thus, corespondence
4150   For our friend Thomas
          Is of whatt we know
        According to the orientation
          Of your finite *modus*
        To Me.
4155   You see, I,
        As the Godhede,
          Am intrinsically
        More knoue-able,
          And yet to you,
4160   In My essence,
          I am Utterly
        Unknouen.
          This means that
        Rather than corespondence

4165   Beyng guaranteed
          In its mesuring of the given,
            As for thinned-owt
          Modern nociouns
            Of correspondence,
4170   It is in-sted guaranteed
          By its conformatioun
          To the divyne well-springinge
            Of the gifte of realite.
          While to advaunce
4175   To-wards this sours*   *source
          Is to advaunce *in unknoueing*,
            It is oonly in terms
          Of this unknoueing,
            Encresed through feith,
4180   That you confyrm even your
            Ordinary knoueing
          Of finyte thyngs.
            More-over, this conformatioun
          To My Divyne Mynde
4185   Is more emphatic in its claim
          Than simply an
            Analogical drawinge-anigh,
          Or resemblaunce.[156]

          MR NO-NONSENSE:
4190   *Heauenes*. Realli?
            Do go on.

          DEUS:
          It is an assimilatioun,
          An ontologicall impresse
4195   Whiche moulds
            Or contryves
          The very formes of thyngs;
            And all this happes,
          As it were,

4200   With-outen youre knoueing it.
        It occurs transparauntly;
            As with the
        Invisible mediatiouns
            Of beauty.
4205   You look
            Throwgh this "makinge"
        With-outen seeing it,
            Even as you knoue
        Biyonde your-selves
4210   By means of it.

        MR NO-NONSENSE:
        So, it rather seems
            That we have foryotten
        That whatt we knoue is
4215   *More* than
        We can possibly knoue.

        DEUS:
        Exactly.
            And, more-over,
4220   Euen when
            You porful unwely fellowes
        Are lookyng at
            Ordinary temporell thyngs,
        Streinyng to be like
4225   Goobet and Me,
        Apprehendinge
            A lunare eclips,[157]
        Euen then,
            At swich a moment of
4230   Lowly endeaver,
            The motiouns of
        Your intellect
            And of your wyll
        Vastly exceed

4235   Your able-hood,
        And mould for-self into
          My Own Idiom of the
        Generaytioun of the
        Eternall Word
4240   From Me, the Fader,
          And of Me, the Holy Spiryt,
        From the Fader and the Sonne.
          Thus, just as Thomas says,
        To correspond
4245   In knoueing
        Is to be conformed
          To the infenite unknouen,
        So lijk-wise,
          Your knoueing of
4250   *Ani-wat at all—*
          How-ever local or mondeine—
        Is in some mezure
          A biforen-sihte*   *advanced sight, prolepsis
        Of the Beatific visioun,
4255   And unioun with the
        Personale interplaie
          Bitwix the persons
        Of the Trilli-hod ... ¹⁵⁸   [*Exit* DEUS *equitando*]

                                              FOL. LVIII R

4260   GOOBET:
        Was thaht really...
          Who I thynke it was?
        But how are we
          To be iwislich* thaht it   *certain
4265   Was not some
          Ffend or phantome?
        Was that trewly
          The divyne worde
        Yt-self spekyng?

4270   THOMAS:
        You cannoughte be sure
            From the visioun alone,
        Yet the visioun
            Is warraunted by
4275   Holy Scripture,
            Whiche records the
        Cominge of
            Trewth yt-self,
        In time,
4280   In human flessh,
        So thaht the
            Infinitlye certeyn trewth
        Coincyded
            With a certeinty
4285   Of whicch you, Goobet,
            Could as readily
        Be sure
            As the certeinty
        Of your fellowes
4290   On the Green.

        GOOBET:
        That's as may be,
            But this walkynge-trewth
        Has never appeared
4295   On my Green
        Bifore todaye.
            How am I to belieue
        A booke that I
            Cannought read?
4300   And how can
            The very realte
        Of trewth
            Dipend on
        Te arryval of
4305   One persoun in tyme?

THOMAS:
But if you were
  Able to read, Goobet,
You would discern
4310   This-very trewth
In the Gospelle of Iohn
  Concernyng Criste,
Synce you would see
  That it contayns
4315 All of naturall
  And super-naturall,
Physicall and
  Metaphysicall wysdom,
As I diclare
4320   In my commentary
On the same.
  But in trewth,
As learnyd,
  I am in no better conditioun
4325 Than you,
  Synce I can oonly
Discern this
  By the presence
Of the seints*   *saints
4330   Who witnesse
Throwgh tyme
  To the comyng
Of the trewth.
  For amongst
4335 Those seints,
  The body of Cryste
Is evenly forscatered,*   *dispersed or scattered in all directions
  As the sense of touche
Through-out the body.[159]
4340   The trewth

Is stille present
   As the Churche
Whiche we
   Palpabully apprehende,
4345   And moste of all
   When we tayste
The trewth
   In the Messe*   *Mass, or Eucharist
And savour it
4350   With our tonges.

GOOBET:
—you mean,
   As I once herde,
"O taste and see..."[160]

4355   THOMAS:
Yes, Goobet, that ys it.
   You may taste
The trewth
   In bred and wyne,
4360   But that is
   But a fore-tayste.
The truewh is
   What we will
One daye see,
4365   Or contemplate,
When we wyll
   Bicome
The very medium
   Ourselves.
4370   Bicause it is
   Beyng yt-self,
It wyl be the mooste
   Palpable thyng of al,
The sensing of som-thyng,

4375   And sensing
         Thaht we sense,
            And then sensing
         Our sensing,
            Whicch is to knoue.
4380   In-wis,
            The Philosophe advyses
         That to say thaht
            God knoues Him-self,
         Is to mean that
4385   He touches Him-self.
         What els could trewth
            Really be,
         When you thynk abowt it?

*[The assembled group suddenly heares voyces singinge, "Sanctus,
Sanctus, Sanctus!" drawing closer and closer]*

4390   MR NO-NONSENSE:
         I need a sherry. *[mopping his brow]*
            Oh thou
         Straunger women!

[Distaunt romble of thonder. Enter DIOTIMA, MONICA *and*
MACRINA *dauncing in a cercle, traycing a spyral with their steppes
as they move closer. The interlocutyrs are uncertayn whether to kneel,
swoone or runne awei.]*[161]

4395   DIOTIMA:
         [still in motion] Sing of Love[162]
            Who takes to Godde
         Your preyeres and repetitiouns!
            Love, who bynds all to-gether,
4400   Love, who lifts your artefacciouns
            Back to Godde![163]
            Love, who is our tragedye
         And our salvacioun!

MACRINA:

4405   Love is all we haue
      On this rownde erth;
    Dolente* Loue!   *grieving, sorrowful
      The souerayne* Treuth,   *sovereign
    Whiche we have long tyme asoght,
4410   Is encercled with
    Oure loue and waimentrie.*   *lamentation.
      All parlay* and all ydeas   *speech
    Are sorwinge* and sikfulle.*[164] *sorrowing *full of sighing
    Ech werde and mot
4415   Yserchen ech*   *each and every
      Lost lif or love,
    And fynds yt-self
      Not allone.
    Reste a-while
4420   Your fatigat* bodies,   *wearied
    Vnder the vine-gert trees,
      Wearyed with the toil
    Of your journey
      To-wardes the Bridegroom![165]
4425   I too
      Was crucifixed
    With Thee! [*stretching out her arms wyde as she dances*][166]
      I takken my flessh
    Thurghdriven
4430   To Thy cross![167]

MONICA:

    [*weeping*] Bryng porrige,
      Waterr, bredde
    And wyne![168]
4435   Moder of the Vertues!
    How my bitere teris*   *bitter tears
      Waterr the grounde
    Every-wher I go![169] [*waves kerchief*]

DIOTIMA:

4440 [*bitterly*] O stop snivelinge, Monica!
          Our daunce transcenden
      The dyadic gaze!
          We generate one an-other
      Through our folwable* steppes;   *imitative, followable
4445   Our "three" is al-so
      "Ffour" and "ffive"!
          As for the seraphim
      Who merge movement
      And sight,
4450 And are al-redy
          At their goal,
      And yet contynuyngly fly,
          There is no visioun of Love
      Without the engendering and
4455   Mouemente of Love,
      Al-times reciprocall,
          Al-wey bynding to-gether,
      With wei-la and joie,
          Unknoueinge and knoueing,
4460 Counterposen parfitly.
          We chaunt, encercle and see! [170]

[*As the three women continue to daunce, the thonderous clouds part,
and* BEATRICE *suddenly appears afar off, on the scaffolde, tornyng
towards* GOOBETT][171]

BEATRICE:
Y-tourn Gobet!*[172]   *turn
4465   What these three see
      Is my smyle!
          Though I more distaunt am
      From you on-the-Grene
          Than the ocean bed
4470 From the height of Cassiopeia,

Still my smyle shaften!*   *sends out long low beams
As the sonne*   *sun
Through a rein-shouwer
And thonder-clapps,
4475   So it scintyllates
Even throwgh
The densest waterrs,
Where the sonne yt-self
Cannot thurgh-reacch.
4480   Lo! It beams throwgh
The welter
Of Monica's sobs,
Akin to Catherine's
Four-folde teares,[173]
4485   Wetter than
Ploungy cloudes,[174]
And the swirling Pacifyc,
Whiche has not yet
Ben ifinden.
4490   My smyle apercen*   *pierces through
The abissus
Of the unknown,
And rechen farther
Than any gaze,
4495   Synce it is the
Visible respounse
To the infenite
Dyvyne enlumining.

[*The daunce continues. All the characters join the dance, includyng those representing non-mistical nociouns, to form a colourful pageant, accompanyed by a certayn amount of braying.* BEATRICE *flies up on cheins and pulleis.*[175] GOBET *stepps forwarde and addresses the assembled threnge.*]

4500   FOL. V LXX

GOOBET:

And so, my Ffrendys,*   *friends
    Through this plesaunt daye,*[176]   *pleasant day
We fynde our Sowle*   *soul
4505   Doth even tarry*   *already tarries
In Paradys,
    Where is restoren
All maner of Thynge,*   *kinds of thing
    With apprailere*   *highly seasoned meat dish
4510   And habernden,*   *salt codfish
    And brimmen*   *brimming clusters of
Bullace bobbes,*[177]   *bullace plums
    Wil al be buxom*   *humble or mild
At God's byddyng:
4515   Here through
Our imaginacioun
    And Goddes' mercye ai,
The Tree that
    Ys of Connyng
4520 Is grown into
The Tree of
Our salvacioun:[178]
    In knowing, al thing
We bynde again,*[179]   *In knowing, all things are bound together
4525   And taaste the lyght
With our fyngeres' towch.[180]
And do vnbotton*   *undo
    Oure kyndes' Falle:[181]
The Trewthe of Gode
4530 And Bee-yng and Beautye
    Xal be tyede,*[182]   *Shall be tied together
And a perfyth of corde*   *And a perfect accord
    Betwyx God and man,*   *Between God and human beings
Whiche trewth xal*   *[From?] which truth shall
4535   Nevyr divide.*[183]   *Never [be] divide[d]

Mannys Sowle
  In blysse
Now xal be edyfyd:*[184]   *be edified
  For ther wyl
4540 Be fruts of prys, pepyr,
    Peon and swete liquoriz,*[185]   *Pepper, the seed of the
                                                    peony, sweet liquorice
  And shortbreds, tartes,
    To ende the
  Wyntry daye;
4545   Pere and Ploume*   *pear and plum
  And other fruites be,
    Rejoice in God,
  *Cuius coelesti mysteris**   *by whose heavenly mystery we receive
    *Pascimur et potamur!**   *food and drink

4550 And so in roundel,[186]
    Festaunce and gloutinge,*   *feasting and guzzling to repletion
  We worshippe Godde
    In gode manere,*   *in good manner
  And shal in hefne*   *heaven
4555   Have endless pes.*   *peace

And so endeth the
BUMPKEEN
PLAIE

NOTES

1 Blotting Paper C. P. Mn. I. 17, c. 46r.

2 Pink ties C. P. Mn. I. 18, c. 46r.

3 Unbound Fragments C. P. Mn. I. 19, c. 46r.

4 Pigeon Hole C. P. Mn. I. 20, c. 46r.

5 Floorboard C. P. Mc. I. 18, c. 46r.

6 Floorboard C. P. Mc. I. 21, c. 46r.

7 G. K. Chesterton, *Saint Thomas Aquinas* (New York, 1956), p. 50.

8 Highbury C. P. Mn. I. 23, c. 46r.

9 No archive numbers are available here, as the Editor has been unable to gain access to the MSS, and has merely heard tell of them. One player in a recent student production claims to have chanced upon the so-called *Bus Shelter* MS whilst travelling on a long journey in Colombia in 2022, but felt it would be indecorous to carry it home in case it was missed by a local band of players.

10 But see Peter Meredith and John E. Tailby (eds.), *The Staging of Religious Drama in Europe in the later Middle Ages: Texts and Documents in English translation* (Kalamazoo: Medieval Institute Publications, 1983), p. 55. See also William Tydeman, "An introduction to medieval English theatre," in Richard Beadle (ed.), *The Cambridge Companion to Medieval English theatre* (Cambridge: Cambridge University Press, 1994), pp. 1–36, p. 1.

11 Ezra Clydebounde, *The Crozier Manuscript* (Oxford: Headington Press, 1980), pp. 96–145. Clydebound attests to a reference in the diary of the vicar of S. Michael's Church, Village of Beer, Parish of Manaton, South Devon, to a performance of the play (D. a 1. 1554) atop Salcombe Hill, Sidmouth, "next the Frog Stone" (situated on the South West Coastal Path, between Sidmouth and the village of Beer, OS Grid Reference OS SY 141877) at All Souls-tide, 1965, seven months after the Stone had been lowered by helicopter from the beach below to its present position as part of an Royal Navy Frigate training mission from HMS Heron, to raise money for the retention of a local cottage hospital. See *Sid Vale Association Magazine* 88 (Summer, 2018), p. 9.

12 V. A. Kolve, *The Play Called* Corpus Christi (Stanford, CA: Stanford University Press, 1966), p. 35.

13 See Michael E. Hoenicke Moore, "Demons and the Battle for Souls at Cluny," *Sciences Religieuses* 32.4 (2003), pp. 485–97.

14 *A Linguistic Atlas of Late Medieval English*, eds. Angus McIntosh, M. L. Samuels and Michael Benskin, 4 vols. (Aberdeen: Aberdeen University Press, 1986).

15 Victor I. Scherb's *Staging Faith: East Anglian Drama in the Later Middle Ages* (London: Associated University Presses, 2001), p. 14, and Nelson (ed.), *Records of Early English.*

16 "Grace, if God will grant us of his great might, | On scaffolds with costumes the roles we will play | This day sevennight, before you in sight | [. . .] on the green in richest array." *The Castle of Perseverance*, ed. David N. Klausner (Kalamazoo: Medieval Institute Publications, 2010), lines 131–34.

17 Meredith and Tailby, eds., *The Staging of Religious Drama*, pp. 71–74; and Sumiko Miyajima, *The Theatre of Man: Dramatic Technique and Stagecraft in the English Medieval Moral Plays*, p. 11.

18 Granger, *The N-Town Play* (p. 1); John C. Coldewey, "The non-cycle plays and the East Anglian tradition," in Beadle, ed., *Cambridge Companion*, pp. 189–210, p. 202.

19 See Scherb, *Staging Faith*, pp. 12–13.

20 Meg Twycross, "The theatricality of medieval English plays," in Beadle, ed., *Cambridge Companion*, pp. 37–84, p. 63.

21 Katja Pilhuj, *Women and Geography on the Early Modern English Stage* (Gendering the Late Medieval and Early Modern World) (Amsterdam: Amsterdam University Press, 2019).

22 Marie de Freluquet, *Que toute chair mortelle se taise: Devenir animal face à l'univocité de l'être* (Tours: Presse Winston, 2000).

23 J. C. Dickinson, *Monastic Life in Medieval England* (London: A. & C. Black, 1961).

24 Tatyana Fitchmeyer, *Gott oder Bumpkin: Was soll es sein?* (Munich: Kühle Bergpresse, 1981).

25 Moses Tremblay, "Qui est Monsieur No-Nonsense ? Au cœur de *Fabula Rustici*," *Etudes de théâtre médiéval obscure* IV. 3 (2012), pp. 344–402.

The reader may find more general theological works on medieval metaphysics a helpful background to the present play. For example, John Milbank and Catherine Pickstock, *Truth in Aquinas* (London: Routledge, 2000), and the present Editor's own *Thomas d'Aquin et la quête eucharistique* (Paris: Editions Ad Solem, 2001).

26 See below, note 35.

27 [*Guild-ascription*] The Guild of All Souls Playe. This may have been a "souling" play.

28 These incomplete details as to costume, in MS annotations [Crozier FR M. a. 172] were excluded from Alan H. Nelson, ed., *Records of Early English Drama: Cambridge*, 2 vols. (Toronto: Toronto University Press, 1989) because their connection with the then extant version of the play, known only as *Fabula Rustici* (FR M. a. 172), could not be established. The costume in the present edition that is indicated for DEUS is one of many signs that the play may be pre-Reformation in origin. Post-Reformation performances of the Chester Play, for example, specified in the Banns that God should not be visibly (en) acted, but that an off-stage voice would speak His lines, for no man may "proportion" to the Godhead. See Frederick Millet Salter and Walter Wilson Greg (Malone Society), *The Trial & Flagellation with Other Studies in the* Chester Cycle (Oxford: Oxford University Press, 1936), p. 159; see also V. A. Kolve, *The Play called* Corpus Christi (Stanford, CA: Stanford University Press, 1996), p. 31. The costumes specified here are not atypical. See Peter Meredith and John Tailby, eds., *The Staging of Religious Drama in Europe in the Later Middle Ages* (Kalamazoo, MI: Western Michigan University Press, 1984), p. 130. Animal parts, specifically tails and ears, are specified, for example, at lines 3560 ff. and 3614. On the use of artificial animal parts, see *Staging*, pp. 117–22.

29 The opening Banns declared by Goobet allocate *The Bumpkin Play* to All Souls' Day; see line 42. Assuming its provenance as indicated at line 1, this play may be non-cyclic; or it may be the only extant portion of a cycle associated with Impyngton (recorded in the Domesday Book as Epintone; also known as Empinton, Ympiton, Impynton, meaning "place belonging to the imps"), now known as Impington, Cambridgeshire.

30 Goobet-on-the-Green [Gobet]C. [Goobett]P. "Goobett-on-the-Greene" calls the Banns at the opening of *The Barbers Playe*, of the Chester Mystery Cycle, line 13 (*The Chester Mystery Cycle: A Facsimile of British*

Library Harley MS 2124, ed. David Mills, *Leeds Texts and Monographs Facsimiles*, 8 [1984]). This connection links the opening of *The Bumpkin Play* with the "folk" play tradition. See *Early English Drama: An Anthology*, ed. John C. Coldwey (New York: Garland Publishing Inc., 1993), p. 325n. However, in *The Barbers Playe*, Goobet speaks only at the opening of the drama, unlike the eponymous character in *The Bumpkin Playe* who enjoys a central role in its dramatic and eschatological dialectic.

31 On the use of Latin in vernacular religious drama, see Penny Granger, *The N-Town Play: Drama and Liturgy in Medieval East Anglia* (Cambridge: D. S. Brewer, 2009), p. 98.

32 *[All hail!]*. Note that the Wakefield *Mactacio Abel* begins with an invocation by Garcio Pikeharnes with a similar interjection: "*All hayll, all hayll, both blithe and glad*," *The Towneley Plays*, ed. George England, EETS, E. S. LXX I (London, 1897). (On the tendency to reductive readings of this play, see C. Davidson, "The Unity of the Wakefield *Mactacio Abel*," *Traditio* 23 (1967), pp. 495-500.) It is not known whether Goobet's opening speech in the present play is an announcement, or "Banns," a "cry" proclaimed a few days in advance of the performance itself, or whether it was an integral part of the play's unified performance. Such a rendering might explain the distinctive versification and diction, with salutation and proclamatory idiom, advertising the coming players and theme, as well as the marked shift to vernacular, and at times demotic diction or even doggerel, as at lines 3560 ff., as well as sometimes unscanned and over-stuffed lines. Alternatively, it may indicate a mixed audience of "unlettered" (e.g. line 420 and lines 1315-17) *hoi polloi* and learned or clerical persons. See William Tydeman, "An introduction to Medieval English Theatre," in Richard Beadle, ed., *The Cambridge Companion to Medieval English Theatre* (Cambridge: Cambridge University Press, 1994), pp. 1-36, p. 23.

33 See Geoffrey Chaucer, *The House of Fame*, ed. F. N. Robinson (Oxford: Oxford University Press, 1988), II. 509.

34 This line attests to a later interpolation, presumably between 1790 and 1936, and tells us something of the identity of players in the past. John Hulse (1708-1790) was an English clergyman from Middlewich. On his death, he bequeathed a large proportion of his estate to establish a prize essay, two scholarships, and the positions of "Hulsean Lecturer" and "Christian Advocate" at the Faculty of Divinity, University of Cambridge. The Hulsean Lecturer was originally required to deliver twenty sermons each year, on the evidence of Christianity or

scriptural difficulties, and the position continues to this day, although the number of lectures has been reduced. In 1860, the Christian Advocate became the "Hulsean Professor of Divinity." In 1934, the Hulsean Professorship was merged with the Norrisian chair, the latter having been founded in 1777 by a bequest from John Norris. Among the original stipulations of the bequest was one particular, that the holder should be between thirty and sixty years old, and that he should be fined twenty-one shillings from his salary if any student attending his lectures was not provided with copies of the Old and New Testaments, and a "Pearson on the Creed." When the two chairs were merged, the expertise of the incumbent was and remains expected to include philosophical theology, although the post does not formally require this.

35 Impington was well-known for two "miraclis": (1) Mrs Elizabeth Woodcock survived seven days buried under a hawthorn bush in heavy snow drifts in 1799, on her way back from selling eggs in Cambridge market: "She was in prison, as you see | All in a cave of snow; | And she could not relieved be, | though she was frozen so. | *Ah, well a-day!* | For she was all froze in with frost, | Eight days and nights, poor soul! | But when they gave her up for lost, | they found her down a hole. | *Ah, well-a-day!*" See William Hone, *The Every-day book and Table Book or Everlasting Calendar of Popular Amusements, Sports, Pastimes, Ceremonies, Manners, Customs, and Events, incident to Each of the three Hundred and Sixty-five Days, in past and present times; forming a complete history of the year, months, and seasons, and a perpetual key to the almanac* (London: Thomas Tegg and Son, 1838), vol. 2, p. 175; and (2) Mr Moses ("Mo") Carter, the so-called Giant (1801–1860), who stood seven feet tall and over twenty-three stone in weight. He lived alone in a hut made of clay hods in Clay Street, and washed himself in Dodd's Pond. He defeated all the boxers at Stourbridge Fair, and for a bet, carried a boulder to Dowst Corner, though it has since been moved to the garden of the Boot Public House, and is still there to this day. The Editor conjectures that the Boot Public House was a sponsor of the dramatic production, or else that it supplied the ale; see H. R. L. Beadle, "The Medieval Drama of East Anglia: Studies in Dialect, Documentary Records and Stagecraft," Ph.D. Thesis, University of York, 1977 (uk.bl.ethos.449288), p. 140.

36 At lines 3–4, Goobet draws upon *The Barbers Playe* of the *Chester Mystery Cycle*. Speculation abounds as to the reason for this textual connection, both in terms of provenance and transmission, as well as geographical non-proximity. But see Eleanor Prosser on the current

critical obsession with anachronistic criteria which propose that religious plays of this period and type are formless, pedantic, sensationalist and estimable only to the extent that they are not religious. Eleanor Prosser, *Drama and Religion in the English Mystery Plays: a re-evaluation* (Stanford, CA: Stanford University Press, 1961), pp. 8-9. See also Maurice Wattle-Sprye, *Textual Interferences in* Fabula Rustici (Blenheim Bridge, Oxon.: Flotsam and Spindrift Press, 1970), pp. 77-95.

37 This line refers to the passing of All Saints' Day, for many years the day before the marking of the Feast of All Souls. The designation of November 1 as the Feast of All Saints developed over time, and does not provide any further clues as to the origin of the present play. Pope Gregory III (731-741) dedicated an oratory in the original S. Peter's Basilica in honour of all the Saints on November 1, and this became the official date for the celebration of the Feast of All Saints in Rome. S. Bede (d. 735) recorded the celebration of All Saints' Day on November 1 in England, and such a celebration also existed in Salzburg, Austria. Ado of Vienne (d. 875) recounted Pope Gregory IV's asking King Louis the Pious (778-840) to proclaim November 1 as All Saints' Day throughout the Holy Roman Empire. Sacramentaries of the ninth and tenth centuries placed the Feast of All Saints on the liturgical calendar on November 1. According to John Beleth (d. 1165), Pope Gregory IV (827-844) officially declared November 1 to be the Feast of All Saints, transferring it from May 13. However, Sicard of Cremona (d. 1215) recorded that Pope Gregory VII (1073-85) suppressed May 13, and mandated November 1 as the date to celebrate the Feast of All Saints. All Souls' Day falls at the opposite end of the year from the season of a-Maying, and this more solemn unfertile season, approaching the "scarce seven hours" of S. Lucy's Day (John Donne, "A Nocturnall upon St Lucy's Day," line 2) may account for the solemnity of theme. See also the reference to summer at line 1447. Ed.

38 Aristotle, *De Anima*, 3. 8. 431b20-21; Aquinas, *Summa Theologiae*, I Q 16.

39 On the correlation of soul and truth, see S. Thomas Aquinas, *Questiones Disputatae de Veritate*, Q 1 and 2 (translated as *Disputed Questions on Truth*, trans. Robert W. Mulligan, S. J. [Chicago: Henry Regnery Company, 1952]).

40 *Quaestiones Disputatae de Veritate*, Q 2 a 5 resp.

41 Aristotle, *De Anima*, 3. 8. 431b 21.

42 An idiomatic opening for this play is to be observed, drawn from the dialogue sung at the beginning of Easter Day Mass, and known for its opening words as the *"Quem queritas"* trope. See Lynette R. Muir, *The Biblical Drama of Medieval Europe* (Cambridge: Cambridge University Press, 1995), p. 13 ff. Is it a *whom* or a *what* that is sought by Goobet? See further William Tydeman, "An introduction to Medieval English Theatre," in Beadle, ed., *The Cambridge Companion to Medieval English Theatre*, 1–36, p. 7.

43 Scholars have noted the myriad linguistic registers of this play, from aureate diction, to vernacular, to slang, often in close proximity. The stage directions are cast in an admixture of sometimes "spliced" Latin and English. This is not unlike other plays of this kind. See Sumiko Miyajima, *The Theatre of Man: Dramatic Technique and Stagecraft in the English Mediaeval Moral Plays* (Clevedon: Clevedon Printing Co., Ltd., 1977), pp. 51 ff.

44 The play's unity revolves around the resolution of the conflict surrounding this question. See Eleanor Prosser, *Drama and Religion in English Mystery Plays: A Re-Evaluation* (Stanford, CA: Stanford University Press, 1961), p. 59.

45 [*pilates*] A discipline of physical fitness developed by Joseph Hubur-tus Pilates (1883–1967). This line attests to a much later interpolation.

46 On gestural references, see Meredith and Tailby, eds., *The Staging of Religious Drama*, pp. 177–83.

47 [francs] The French franc was a gold coin issued in 1360. It became the national currency in France from 1795 until 1999.

48 One of several curiously prophetic references. Ed.

49 A reference to a device for removing dust or debris by suction, named after the Hoover Company, founded in 1908. The proper noun is often used as a verb. This is a much later accretion, testifying to the play's circulation in the later modern period at a time when almost every Western household had a Hoover of its own. Ed.

50 This may be a mollifying indirect reference to the audience, who, in close proximity to the academic disputants of Cambridge, may have been sensitive to their contrasting estate, and suspicious of University affairs. In addition, these plays may have been intended as *"quike* [living] *bookis"* for the unlearned. See John Wycliffe, "A Sermon against Miracle Plays," Eduard Mätzner, ed., *Altenglische Sprachproben,*

I, Part II (Berlin, 1869), pp. 222–42, p. 234 (8). There are references throughout the play to "learned doctors" and "unlettered bumpkins." E.g. lines 420 and 1254.

51 On the problematic status of laughter, see Kolve, *The Play Called Corpus Christi*, pp. 124 ff. See also Hans-Jurgen Diller, "Laughter in Medieval English Drama: A critiquing of Modernizing and Historical Analyses," *Comparative Drama* 36 (2002), pp. 1–19.

52 Interjections and expletives are commonly associated with religious drama of this period, and arguably enjoy a Biblical origin, where Jesus is reviled as a robber, and was mocked. See J. W. Robinson, *Studies in Fifteenth-Century Stagecraft* (Kalamazoo, MI: Western Michigan University, 1991), p. 41. They are features of the "festive." See Warren Edminster, *The Preaching Fox: Festive Subversion in the Plays of the Wakefield Master* (London: Routledge, 2005), p. 45 ff., and Matilda Mooncalf, "Goobet's kenosis: *Fabula Rustici* as a Biblical play after all?" *Études en matière médiévale* 23.6 (2001), pp. 871–99.

53 Diller, "Laughter in Medieval English Drama."

54 [having a practical aspect]. Fran O'Rourke, *Pseudo-Dionysius and the Metaphysics of Aquinas* (Leiden: E. J. Brill, 1992). See also Graham Priest, *Beyond the Limits of thought* (Cambridge: Cambridge University Press, 1995), pp. 130–32.

55 [nowhere]. This Anglo-Saxon remnant is suggestive of a much earlier *Bumpkin Play* tradition, unless it is intended for the reader or audience to be fooled into thinking so. Ed.

56 Derived from The Right Honourable, the Lady Margaret Countess of Newcastle (Margaret Cavendish), "Of Many Worlds in This World," POEMS, AND FANCIES WRITTEN (London: T. R. for J. Martin, and J. Allestrye at the Bell in Saint Pauls Church Yard, 1653), Part I, lines 5–10.

57 Derived from The Right Honourable, the Lady Margaret Countess of Newcastle, "What *Atomes* make the *Sun*, and the *Sea*, go round," from *Nature calls a Councell, which was Motion, Figure, matter*, and *Life*, to advise about making the World. POEMS, AND FANCIES WRITTEN, lines 1–7.

58 See Robert Greville, *The Nature of Christ* [1640], facsimile reprint (London: Gregg International, 1969), p. 39.

59 See Anne Conway, *The Principles of the Most Ancient and Modern Philosophy* (Cambridge: Cambridge University Press, 1996), pp. 56–62.

60 In [Floorboard C. P. Mc. I. 21, c. 46r.], tucked behind the hair side of this page, a highly decorated semi-circular sheet of very thick vellum, of uncertain date, was found by a research student in 1999, now catalogued in Emmanuel College, and on occasional display in the Museum of College Life. It resembles a galette flatbread in form and pigment, and bears the signature of the British Post-War and contemporary artist, "O. Soskice." It is thought to be a stage prop for Thomas to carry on to the stage, following this rubric.

61 Giorgio Agamben, *State of Exception*, trans. Kevin Attell (Chicago: Chicago University Press, 2005).

62 Much ink has been spilled on this three-word phrase and its prophetic anticipation of, or influence upon the British poet John James (b. 1939), . . . *mmm . . . ah yes* (London: Ferry Press, 1967). For a summary of scholarly treatments of this question, see Wattle-Sprye, *Textual Interferences*, pp. 2301-7.

63 *Quaestiones Disputatae de Veritate*, Q 1 a. 1.

64 *Quaestiones Disputatae de Veritate*, Q 1 a 1 resp; see also Q 1 a. 4 resp. V. J. Bourke, trans., *Disputed Questions on Truth* (Chicago, IL: Chicago University Press, 1952-54).

65 Augustine, *De Trinitate* Book IX. See also Thomas Aquinas, *De Ente et Essentia*, IV 2.

66 *Quaestiones Disputatae de Veritate*, Q 1 a 1 resp; Q 22 a 1 ad 12; *Summa Theologiae*, I–II Q 27 a 1 ad 3. See also Rudi te Velde, *Participation and Substantiality in Thomas Aquinas* (London: E. J. Brill, 1995).

67 A possible indication of stagecraft. See Robinson, *Studies in Fifteenth-Century Stagecraft*, p. 24; Meredith and Tailby, eds., *The Staging of Religious Drama*, p. 71.

68 In this line, an implicit comparison is drawn between Mesopotamia in Oxford, a narrow ait measuring eight hundred yards by thirty yards that forms part of the University Parks, lying between the upper and lower levels of the River Cherwell which are partly interspersed with tributaries of the River Thames, and the region of Western Asia, situated within the Tigris Euphrates river system, in the northern part of the Fertile Crescent, today roughly corresponding to most of Iraq, Kuwait, the eastern parts of Syria, Southeastern Turkey, and regions along the Turkish–Syrian and Iran–Iraq borders. This geographical comparison corresponds with the philosophical

influence referred to at lines 898-920. The geographical interspersing of narrow aits of land between various rivers echoes the metaphysical deictic complexity of *ens commune*, as "biyond | All hierarchicall qualificatiouns" (lines 903-4).

69 *Liber de Causis* (Milwaukee WI: Marquette University Press, 1984).

70 *Summa Theologiae*, I Q 5 a 1-3.

71 [L. *digitalis*] and [L. *Capsella bursa-pastoris*]

72 [hedgerow flowers]

73 For such a theory, any claims that phrases "truly" correspond reduce to mere statements that "such and such is the case," this being in effect another way of saying that metaphysical questions about a supposed solemn mystery named "truth" need deflating in favour of considering the conditions of "warranted assertibility." See Gottlob Frege, "On Concept and Object" [1892], *Translations from the Philosophical Writings of Gottlob Frege*, eds. Peter Geach and Max Black (Oxford: Basil Blackwell, 1960), 42-55; "The thought: A Logical Inquiry," *Mind* 65, 259 (July, 1956), 289-311; F. P. Ramsey, "Facts and Propositions," *Proceedings of the Aristotelian Society* Supplementary Volume 7 (1927), 153-70; A. J. Ayer, "The Criterion of Truth," *Analysis* 3 (1935), 28-32; W. V. O. Quine, *Philosophy of Logic* (Englewood Cliffs, NJ: Prentice Hall, 1970); Donald Davidson, "The Structure and Content of Truth," *The Journal of Philosophy* 87. 6 (1990), 279-326; Matthew McGrath, *Between Deflationism and Correspondence* (New York: Garland Publishing, 2000).

74 *Quaestiones Disputatae de Veritate*, Q 1 a 1 resp; *Summa Theologiae*, I-II Q 27 a 1 ad 3.

75 Presumably this refers to those ancient thinkers mentioned at lines 1044-59 known for their pursuing of philosophical clarity. Ed.

76 Velde, *Participation*, p. 273.

77 Aquinas, *Quaestiones Disputatae de Veritate*, Q 1 a 1 resp. See also Q 2 a 11 resp. See also *Summa Theologiae*, I Q 5; I-II-ae Q 27 a 1 ad 3.

78 *Quaestiones Disputatae de Veritate*, Q 1 a 1 resp.

79 *Quaestiones Disputatae de Veritate*, Q 1 a 1 resp. Truth is the *convenantiam unius entis ad aliud*. That *convenientia* is the ontological ground of analogy is shown at Q 1 a 11 resp.

₈₀ Concerning the verb "to square," see F. M. Cornford, *Microcos-mographia Academica: Being a Guide for the Young Academic Politician* (Cambridge: Bowes & Bowes, 1908), IX: "IX SQUARING: this most important branch of political activity is, of course, closely connected with *Jobs*. These fall into two classes, My Jobs and Your Jobs. My Jobs are public-spirited proposals, which happen (much to my regret) to involve the advancement of a personal friend, or (still more to my regret) of myself. Your Jobs are insidious intrigues for the advancement of yourself and your friends, speciously disguised as public-spirited proposals. The term Job is more commonly applied to the second class. When you and I have, each of us, a Job on hand, we shall proceed to go on the Square. [. . .] Squaring can be carried on at lunch; but it is better that we should meet casually. The proper course to pursue is to walk, between 2 and 4 p.m., up and down the King's Parade, and more particularly that part of it which lies between the Colleges of Pembroke and Caius. When we have succeeded in meeting acciden-tally, it is etiquette to talk about indifferent matters for ten minutes and then part. After walking five paces in the opposite direction, you should call me back, and begin with the words, 'Oh, by the way, if you should happen [. . .]' The nature of Your Job must then be vaguely indicated, without mentioning names; and it should be treated by both parties as a matter of very small importance. You should hint that I am a very influential person, and that the whole thing is a secret between us. Then we shall part as before, and I shall call you back and introduce the subject of My Job, in the same formula. By observing this procedure, we shall emphasise the fact that there is *no connection whatever* between my supporting your Job and your supporting mine. This absence of connection is the essential feature of Squaring. [. . .] Remember this: *the men who get things done are the men who walk up and down King's Parade, from two to four, every day of their lives.* You can either join them, and become a powerful person; or you can join the great throng of those who spend all their time in preventing them from getting things done, and in the larger task of preventing one another from doing anything whatever. This is the Choice of Hercules, when Hercules takes to politics."

₈₁ See lines 887 ff. and 1043 ff.

₈₂ The following MSS omit the entry of the Wife of Bath altogether, lines 1304-12: [Crozier MSS FR M. a. 172] [Crozier II D. a l. 1554] [Blot-ting Paper C. P. Mn. I. 17] [Pink Ties c. 46r., C. P. Mn. I. 18 c. 46r.] and [Unbound Fragments C. P. Mn. I. 19, c. 46r.]. Questions abound as to

the significance of this passage. Do the laden baskets anticipate the
"fruts of prys" in Goobet's closing *paean* (line 4540)? Is she rushing to
the end of the play to furnish that closing feast? One notes that the
Wife of Bath's rather sudden and anti-clerical intervention may under-
line the concern expressed at lines 890, 1043 ff., 1287 ff., 1950 about
"strange doctrines" brewing at Oxford, or may represent the circulation
of ideas concerning the perceived corruption of the clerical orders in
general, for their excessive worldliness, as well as their rarefied discourses. Inversely, she is associated with cautioning against attending
"a someres game" (see *The Wife of Bath's Prologue*, line 654). However,
the Wife of Bath's intervention in *The Bumpkin Play* has licensed some
scholars to speculate whether this play displays conventions of "festive
disorder," as, for example, with the plays of the Wakefield Master. See
the scabrous low-life scene (Act Three, Scene Two), before the entry
of DEUS; the absurd pseudo-philosophical banter about currants and
puddings might be situated within the commonplace of carnival dis-
may, but also invertedly to anticipate the festal Eucharistic theme at
the closing of the play (lines 4345-50). Certainly, no end of scholars
has taken the opportunity to speculate as to the Wife of Bath's curious
inclusion in some versions of the play. See Edminster, *The Preaching
Fox*, pp. 4-5. Some scholars have noted the theological or liturgical, as
opposed to Biblical, theme of the present play, as suggestive of clerical
authorship, perhaps in opposition to the arguably under-represented
clerical distrust voiced by the Wife of Bath. See Lauren Lepow, *Enacting the Sacrament* (Rutherford: Fairleigh Dickinson University Press,
1990), p. 28, and Mikhail Bakhtin, *Rabelais and his World*, trans. Helene
Iswolsky (Bloomington, IN: Indiana University Press, 1984), pp. 7-21.
See also Kolve, *The play called Corpus Christi*, p. 136 ff., and Tydeman,
"An introduction," in Beadle, ed., *Cambridge Companion*, p. 11. This
interpretative oscillation in existing scholarship should prompt one
not to look too closely for a single viewpoint or unifying authorial
stance. Indeed, it may be an example of what Mikhail Bakhtin has
described as "heteroglossia that had been dialogized": Mikhail Bakhtin,
The Dialogic Imagination, trans. Caryl Emerson and Michael Holquist
(Austin, TX: University of Texas Press, 1981), p. 273.

83 Geoffrey Chaucer, *The Wife of Bath's Tale*, lines 857-81.

84 Scholars are unable to establish the significance of these material items, except to attribute them to the primitive realism "of a
charming but simple people." See Prosser, *Drama and Religion*, p. 14.
Turnips were sometimes hollowed out to make "souling" lanterns,

to be carried about by soulers on the night before All Souls' Day, when the veil between life and death was at its thinnest; the turnip lanterns would protect the soulers from spirits such as Stingy Jack, the legendary figure who offered his soul to the Devil in exchange for one last drink. See also lines 3565 ff. for a possible reference to soul-mass cakes (see n. 149).

85 [late mornings 9-12; mornings] *The Wife of Bath's Tale*, lines 874-75.

86 Stephen R. L. Clark, *The Moral Status of Animals* (Oxford: Oxford University Press, 1977).

87 The Incipit of a medieval English round of the mid-thirteenth century; it is also known as the Summer Canon or Cuckoo Song. One notes a further reference to weather and the seasons.

88 *Summa Theologiae*, I Q 5 a 4 ad 1; Ia-IIae Q 27 a 1 ad 3.

89 Implying that there may be countless other mysteriously unknown transcendentals besides? Ed.

90 A further climatic reference. It is such a recurrent theme in this play that either one must assume that the players are more accustomed to other climates and find (like Thomas) the local weather systems to be bothersome; or, one may attribute to these medieval individuals that same tendency to discuss the weather incessantly as is often invoked as a caricature of daily discourses between British subjects.

91 *Tota pulchra es* is an old Catholic prayer, written in the fourth century. It is one of the five antiphons for the psalms of Second Vespers for the Feast of the Immaculate Conception. The words "You are all beautiful" refer to the Virgin Mary, and in this line may anticipate the approach of mystical women at line 4462 ff., and especially Beatrice.

92 Henri Pouillon, "La Beauté, Propriété Trancendentale chez les Scolastiques, 1220-1270," *Archives d'histoire doctrinale et littéraire du Moyen Age* XV (1946), pp. 263-328; Georges Bernanos, *The Diary of a Country Priest*, trans. Pamela Morris (New York: Carroll and Graf Publishers, 1937, 1965).

93 "Beauty and goodness in a thing are identical fundamentally; for they are based upon the same thing, namely, the form; and consequently, goodness is praised as beauty. But they differ logically, for goodness properly relates to the appetite (goodness being what all things desire); and therefore, it has the aspect of an end (the appetite

being a kind of movement towards a thing). On the other hand, beauty relates to the cognitive faculty; for beautiful things are those which please when seen. Hence beauty consists in due proportion; for the senses delight in things duly proportioned, as in what is after their own kind – because even sense is a sort of reason, just as is every cognitive faculty. Now, since knowledge is by assimilation, and similarity relates to form, beauty properly belongs to the nature of a formal cause." *Summa Theologiae*, I Q 5 a 5 ad 1.

94 See further E. de Bruyne, *Études d'aesthetique médiévale* (Louvain: Éditions de l'Institut Supérieur de Philosophie, 1946); Umberto Eco, *The Aesthetics of Thomas Aquinas*, trans. Hugh Bredin (London: Radius, 1988); Gilbert Narcisse OP, *Les Raisons de Dieu: Arguments de convenance et esthétique théologie selon St Thomas d'Aquin et Hans Urs von Balthasar* (Fribourg: Editions Universitaires Fribourg Suisse, 1997), especially pages 184-92.

95 John Donne, *The Litanie*, IV.29. This is the sixth prophetic allusion of the play, noted by scholars, and much debated. See Eric Mayheme, *Prophetic Invocations in the* Impyngton Plaiye (Mayfair, London: Uppity Press, 1978), vol. 1, p. 431. Ronald Dilly-Dilly poses a savage critique of Mayheme's account of festive prophecy in medieval comic drama in his ground-breaking essay, "A Response to Mayheme: Solemn Prolepsis in Low-Life Scenes," *Elliptika* 2 (1998), 677-712.

96 *Quaestiones Disputatae de Veritate*, Q 1 a 1 resp.

97 This line anticipates Act Three, Scene Two.

98 Floorboard C. P. Mc. I. 21, c. 46r. is the only MS in which this textual prolepsis is to be found.

99 *Quaestiones Disputatae de Veritate*, Q 1 a 2; *Summa Theologiae*, Q 1 a 2, a 3, a 5; Q 14 a 16; Q 15 a 2 ad 2; Q 16 a 6.

100 Thomas is referring to Ibn Sina. See Stanislas Breton, " La deduction thomiste des catégories," *Revue Philosophique de Louvain*, third Series, vol. 60, no. 65 (1962), pp. 5-32.

101 *Quaestiones Disputatae de Veritate*, Q 4 a 2 resp; Q 10 a 1 resp.

102 This may refer to the vote which took place in Cambridge University to decide whether to award the philosopher, M. Jacques Derrida, an honorary degree on 16 May 1992. Although the proposal to award him the degree was challenged, and much shouting and braying took

place between members of the opposite queues, when the dons voted, the *placets* ("it pleases me") outvoted the *non-placets* by 336 to 204. The United Kingdom Independence Party was founded in 1993, a year after the "Dreaded Queue." But this is all-souling season, when disparate chronotopic occurences enjoy inexplicable simultaneity.

103 [perfection]

104 *De Ente et Essentia*, IV 2.

105 Oliva Blanchette, *The Perfection of the Universe According to Aquinas: A teleological cosmology* (University Park, PA: Pennsylvania State University Press, 1992).

106 Aristotle, *De Anima*, 3. 8. 431b 21; Aquinas, *Quaestiones Disputatae de Veritate*, Q 1 a 1; Q 2 a 2.

107 *Quaestiones Disputatae de Veritate*, Q 2 a 2.

108 Festive expression typically includes examples drawn from the natural order, the seasons or elements; one can also note references to village greens, festival days of the liturgical calendar and times of day, all of which pertain in this play. See C. L. Barber, *Shakespeare's Festive Comedy* (Princeton, NJ: Princeton University Press, 1959), pp. 5–6; see also John Wesley Harris, *Medieval theatre in Context* (New York: Routledge, 1992), p. 58; see also Mayheme, *Prophetic Invocations*, and Dilly-Dilly, "A Response."

109 Wladyslaw Tatarkiewicz, *History of Aesthetics* (Mouton: De Gruyter Mouton, 1970), vol. 1, pp. 276 ff.

110 See Mayheme, *Prophetic Invocations*, Vol. 2, p. 224.

111 This may be an allusion to the vellum or reinforced parchment prop of a gallet flatbread which Thomas carries on to the stage at his first entry (line 631; see also lines 2097–98).

112 *Quaestiones Disputatae de Veritate*, Q 1 a 1; a 3; a 5.

113 A sudden change of idiom is a commonplace in drama of this period and genre. See Robinson, *Studies*, p. 42. Modern readers may find the central passages (especially *Fol. 4 – Fol. 14*) somewhat grinding in their pedantic discussions of God's knowing of singulars and the question of where truth is to be found. However, see Twycross, "The theatricality," in Beadle, ed., *Cambridge Companion*, on medieval "staying power in the face of both entertainment and edification," p. 45.

114 "A craftsman is said to produce a false work if it falls short of the proper operation of his art . . . . Something that begets a false opinion is false," thus, "gall is false honey, and tin, false gold," *Summa Theologiae*, I Q 17 a 1 resp.

115 "Natural things are said to be true in so far as they express the likeness of the species that are in the divine mind. For a stone is called true, which possesses the nature proper to the stone, according to the preconception in the divine intellect," *Summa Theologiae*, I Q 16 a 1 resp. See also *Quaestiones Disputatae de Veritate*, Q 1 a 2 resp.

116 *Quaestiones Disputatae de Veritate*, Q 1 a 8: "But negations or privations existing outside the soul do not have any form by which they can imitate the model of divine art or introduce a knowledge of themselves into the human intellect."

117 "For this reason, a thing is said to be true principally because of its order to the truth of the divine intellect rather than because of its relation to the truth of a human intellect," *Quaestiones Disputatae de Veritate*, Q 1 a 4. "All this is entirely from God, because both the very form of a thing, through which it is conformed, is from God, and the truth itself, insofar as it is itself the good of the intellect, as is said in the *Ethics*; for any good of any thing whatsoever consists in its perfect operation. But since the perfect operation of the intellect consists in its knowing the true, that is its good in the sense just mentioned. Hence, since every good and every form is from God, one must say, without any qualification, that every truth is from God," *Quaestiones Disputatae de Veritate*, Q 1 a 8.

118 This reference to play-acting indicates that the *Bumpkin* playwright(s) was (or were) not oblivious to the irony of representing the search for truth in dramatic form. See Saint Augustine, *Soliloquies*, II.x (*Patrologia Latina* 32, ed. J. P. Migne [1861], p. 893) on seeking two-faced truth. However, the evocation of love and feasting later in the play might be seen to correspond with Augustine's understanding of the importance of ripening the mind for the reception of truth; see *Confessiones*, III.2 and *De Doctrina Christiana*, 2:18.54. The pedagogic role of drama, and the deployment of visual and material images in the Middle Ages, deserve mention, as especially linked with the soul's use of the imagination in achieving unity of thought. See Aristotle, *De Anima*, 3.8; and see Theodore K. Lerud, *Memory, Images and the English Corpus Christi Drama* (New York: Palgrave Macmillan, 2008), pp. 36–37.

119 *Quaestiones Disputatae de Veritate*, Q 1 a 2; *Summa Theologiae*, I Q 1 a 4 resp; Q 16 a 1.

120 It is from within the idea of God's unified and simple understanding of Himself that one is pointed to diversity. This is demonstrated by the question of whether there can be a perfect copy of God. Such a copy would, like God, have to be one. From the idea of God's self-understanding as unified act, one is directed towards Trinitarian diversity. See *Quaestiones Disputatae de Veritate*, Q 2 a 1 resp: "If there were anything that could perfectly represent God, that thing would be unique, for it would represent Him in one way and according to one form. For this reason, there is in God only one Son, who is the perfect image of the Father."

121 "As is clear from what has been said, among created things truth is found both in things and in intellect. In the intellect it is found according to the conformity which the intellect has with the things whose notions it has. In things it is found according as they imitate the divine intellect, which is their measure – as art is the measure of all products of art. . . . By its form a thing existing outside the soul imitates the art of the divine intellect; and, by the same form, it is such that it can bring about a true apprehension in the human intellect. Through this form, moreover, each and every thing has its act of existing. Consequently, the truth of existing things includes their entity in its intelligible character, adding to this a relation of conformity to the human or divine intellect," *Quaestiones Disputatae de Veritate*, Q 1 a 8. "But since God infinitely exceeds the power of our intellect, any form we conceive cannot completely represent the divine essence, but merely has, in some small measure, an imitation of it. Similarly, extramental realities imitate it somewhat, but imperfectly. Hence, all different things imitate God in different ways; and, according to different forms, they represent the one simple form of God, since in His form are found perfectly united all the perfections that are found, distinct and multiple, among creatures," *Quaestiones Disputatae de Veritate*, Q 2 a 2. It is hard to miss the irony of this line, given the presence of human actors or copiers, signs that pretend not to be signs, and the thematic implications of these lines for the centrality of *imitatio Christi*. See W. J. T. Mitchell, *Iconology: Image, Text, Ideology* (Chicago: Chicago University Press, 1986), p. 43; see also Edgar Schell, *Strangers and Pilgrims: From* The Castle of Perseverance *to* King Lear (Chicago: Chicago University Press, 1983), pp. 2–10, pp. 13 ff. The thematization and theological justification of imitation may help to safeguard the

players against the risk of blasphemy, especially the player assuming the role of DEUS. See Kolve, *The Play called* Corpus Christi, p. 9. See also Tydeman, "An introduction," in Beadle, ed., *Cambridge Companion*, pp. 5-6, on the complexity of verisimilitude in medieval drama.

122 This judgement is a matter of recognising a thing insofar as it is an imitation of God. See *Quaestiones Disputatae de Veritate*, Q 1 a 3 resp; a 4 resp. Even divine inner illumination requires judgement. See *Summa Theologiae*, I Q 12 a 11 ad 3; Q 79 a 9.

123 "But again, tell me this. It is clear that many wild animals easily surpass human beings in strength and in other physical abilities. What is it in virtue of which a human being is superior, so that he can command many wild animals, yet none of them commands him? Is it not perhaps what we usually call reason or understanding?" Saint Augustine, *De libero arbitrio*, trans. Peter King (Cambridge: Cambridge University Press, 2010), 1.7.16.55. "That by which humans are ranked above animals, whatever it is, be it more correctly called 'mind' or 'spirit' or both — we find both terms in Scripture — if it dominates and commands the rest of what a human consists in, then that human being is completely in order," 1.8.18.61.

124 "We recognize that we share many common characteristics not only with animals but with trees and plants too. We see that taking bodily nutrition, growing, reproducing, and flourishing are also attributes of trees, and are contained in a lower level of life. We also note that wild animals are able to see, hear, and sense material objects by smell or taste or touch. We admit that their senses are often sharper than ours. Add to this energy, vigor, strength in arms and legs, the swiftness and agility of bodily movements: In all these qualities we are superior to some animals, equal to others, and even surpassed by some. Nevertheless, qualities of this sort are surely shared by human beings and animals, despite the fact that every action in an animal's life is pursuing physical pleasures and avoiding discomforts. There are other features that seem not to occur among animals but are not the highest attributes in human beings. Take joking and laughing. Anyone judging human nature most rightly holds that these features are indeed human, but the least important part of a human being. Next, there is the love of praise and of glory, and the drive to dominate. Although absent in animals, we should not be thought better than animals because we lust after these things. When the pursuit of these things is not controlled by reason it makes us unhappy, and no one ever thought to rank himself above others on account of unhappiness.

Thus a human being should be called 'in order' when these selfsame impulses of the soul are dominated by reason. For it should not be called the right order, or even 'order' at all, when the better are controlled by the worse." Augustine, *De Libero Arbitrio*, 1.8.18.61–1.8.18.64.

125 *Summa Theologiae*, I Q 5 a 5 ad 1.

126 Elkanah Settle (1648–1724), known as "Secresie's Song," *The Fairy-Queen* by Henry Purcell, Z. 629/13.

> "One charming night
> Gives more delight
> Than a hundred lucky days:
> Night and I improve the taste,
> Make the pleasure longer last
> A thousand, thousand several ways."

127 *Summa Theologiae*, I Q 14 aa 5–6.

128 *Summa Theologiae*, I Q 77 a 1.

129 Alain de Libera, *Archéologie du Sujet 1: Naissance du Sujet* (Paris: Vrin, 2007), pp. 303–41.

130 Thomas Aquinas, *De Ente et Essentia*, IV 2.

131 "God is said to be in a thing in two ways; in one way after the manner of an efficient cause; and thus He is in all things created by Him; in another way He is in things as the object of operation is in the operator; and this is proper to the operations of the soul, according as the thing known is in the one who knows; and the thing desired in the one desiring. In this second God is especially in the rational creature, which knows and loves Him actually or habitually. And because the rational creature possesses this prerogative by grace, as will be shown later (Q 12), He is thus said to be in saints by grace," *Summa Theologiae*, I Q 8 a 3.

132 Blanchette, *The Perfection of the Universe according to Thomas Aquinas: A teleological ontology*.

133 On profanity in mediaeval religious drama, see Edminster, *The Preaching Fox*, pp. 181–83.

134 "As proof of this, note that the divine knowledge which God has of things can be compared to the knowledge of an artist, since He is the cause of all things as art is the cause of all works of art," *Quaestiones Disputatae de Veritate*, Q 2 a 5 resp. "Now, in order that a thing

be known, its likeness must be in the knower, though it need not be in him in the same manner as it is in reality. Hence our intellect does not know singulars, because the knowledge of these depends upon matter, and the likeness of matter is not in our intellect. It is not because the likeness of a singular is in our intellect in an immaterial way. The divine intellect, however, can know singulars, since it possesses a likeness of matter, although in an immaterial way," *Quaestiones Disputatae de Veritate*, Q 2 a 5 resp.

135 See Pierre-Noël Mayaud, ed., *Le Problème de L'Individuation* (Paris: Vrin, 1991), especially the essays by Bruno Pinchard and Olivier Boulnois.

136 *Quaestiones Disputatae de Veritate*, Q 2 a. 5.

137 "Therefore, others, such as Avicenna and his followers, have said that God knows every singular, but universally, as it were, in knowing all the universal causes from which a singular is produced. An astronomer, for example, knowing all the motions of the heavens and the distances between the celestial bodies, would know every eclipse that will occur even for the next hundred years, yet he would not know any one eclipse as a distinct singular so as to have evidential knowledge that it actually exists or not – which a country bumpkin has when he sees an eclipse. It is in this manner, they say, that God knows singulars," *Quaestiones Disputatae de* Veritate, Q 2 a 5 resp. Are we to see Goobet-on-the-Grene as the Lord of Misrule, who appears in order to replace the usual authorities? Or are the "usual authorities" being implicitly undermined by the adroit wisdom of this unlettered yokel? See Edminster, *The Preaching Fox*, p. 11.

138 A reference to festive stagecraft. See Miriam Plankton, "The Staging of the Impyngton Play(s)," *The Ohio Journal of Medieval Theatre* 29.1 (March, 1971), pp. 402–99, especially p. 453.

139 *Quaestiones Disputatae de Veritate*, Q 4 a 1 resp. See also *Summa Theologiae*, Q 85 a 1 ad 4; a 2 ad 3; Q 79 a 4.

140 Aquinas, *De Potentia*, 9.9. On the *quaestio disputata* concerning Aquinas's continuous adhesion to the truth of things besides the truth of judgement in the mind, see John Milbank, "Manifestation and Procedure: Trinitarian Metaphysics after Albert the Great and Thomas Aquinas," in Marco Salvioli OP, ed., *Tomismo Creativo: letture Contemporanee del* Doctor Communis (Bologna: ESD, 2015), pp. 41–117, p. 108, n. 140.

141 *Quaestiones Disputatae de Veritate*, Q 4 a 1 resp; Q 4 a 2; *Summa Contra Gentiles*, ed. and trans. Joseph Kenny, OP (New York: Hanover House, 1955–57), 4. 11 (6): "Now, I mean by the 'intention understood' what the intellect conceives in itself of the thing understood. To be sure, in us this is neither the thing which is understood nor is it the very substance of the intellect. But it is a certain likeness of the thing understood conceived in the intellect, and which the exterior words signify. So, the intention itself is named the 'interior word' which is signified by the exterior word. Indeed, that the intention aforesaid is not within us the thing understood is clear from this: It is one thing to understand a thing, and another to understand the intention itself, yet the intellect does so when it reflects on its own work; accordingly, some sciences are about things, and others are about intentions understood. Now, that the intention understood is not the very intellect within us is clear from this: the act of being of the intention understood consists in its very being understood; the being of our intellect does not so consist; its being is not its act of understanding"; 4. 11 (16): [16]: "However, things have images of two kinds. For there is an image which does not share the nature with that whose image it is: whether it be its image in respect to the exterior accidents (a bronze statue is the image of a man, yet is not, for all that, a man); or if it be an image in respect of the thing's substance, for the essence of man in the intellect is not a man. The reason, as the Philosopher says, is that 'it is not the stone which is present in the soul, but the species of the stone.' But the image of a thing which has the same nature with that whose image it is is like the son of a king: in him the image of his father appears and he is the same in nature as his father. Now, it was shown that the Word of God is the image of the speaker in respect of His very essence and that the Word has the very nature in common with the speaker. The conclusion, therefore, is that the Word of God is not only the image, but also the Son. For so to be one's image as to be of the same nature with him is not discovered in one who cannot be called a son – so long as we are speaking of living things. For that which proceeds from a living thing in the likeness of species is called son. Hence, we read in a Psalm (2:7): 'The Lord hath said to Me: You are My Son.'" See also *Summa Contra Gentiles*, 4. 12; *Summa Theologiae*, I–II Q 93 a 1 ad 2; I Q 85 a 2 ad 2; I Q 34 a 2 resp.

142 *Quaestiones Disputatae de Veritate*, Q 4 a 2 resp: "Now, for us every object of understanding really proceeds from something else. For example, conceptions of conclusions proceed from principles, conceptions

of the quiddities of later things proceed from quiddities of things prior, or at least an actual conception proceeds from habitual knowledge. Now, this is universally true of whatever we understand, whether it be understood by its essence or by its likeness; for conception itself is an effect of the act of understanding. Consequently, when the mind understands itself, its conception is not the mind but something expressed by the mind's act of knowledge. Hence, two things pertain to the nature of our intellectual word: it is understood, and it is expressed by an agent distinct from itself."

143 Aristotle, *Metaphysics*, Book Θ, chapter six: 1048b18–35.

144 On self-expression as a contained emanation and as craft-like, see *Quaestiones Disputatae de Veritate*, Q 4 a 1 resp: "Consequently, just as we consider three things in the case of a craftsman, namely, the purpose of his work, its model, and the work now produced, so also do we find a threefold word in one who is speaking. There is the word conceived by the intellect, which, in turn, is signified by an exterior vocal word. The former is called *the word of the heart*, uttered but not vocalized. Then there is that upon which the exterior word is modeled; and this is called *the interior word* which has an image of the vocal word. Finally, there is the word expressed exteriorly, and this is called *the vocal word. Now*, just as a craftsman first intends his end, then thinks out the form of his product, and finally brings it into existence, so also, in one who is speaking, the word of the heart comes first, then the word which has an image of the oral word, and, finally, he utters the vocal word." See also *Summa Theologiae*, II–II Q 79 a 9 resp: "For the act of reason is, as it were, a movement from one thing to another."

145 An indication of scaffold use? If so, one might entertain the possibility that such vertical axes foreshadow the eventual exaltation of even apparently mistaken characters. See Plankton, "The Staging of the *Bumpkin Play(s)*," p. 260; Robinson, *Studies*, pp. 23 ff.; See Miyajima, *The Theatre of Man: Dramatic Technique and Stagecraft in the English Mediaeval Moral Plays*, p. 45. See n. 96 and n. 115 on eschatological implications. On the nature of theatrical scaffolds and wagons, see Meg Twycross, "The theatricality of medieval English plays," in Beadle, ed., *Medieval English Theatre*, pp. 37–84.

146 See further, Thomas Aquinas, *Commentary on Aristotle's* Physics, trans. Richard J. Blackwell, Richard J. Spath and Th. Edmund Thirkel (New Haven: Yale University Press, 1963), II. 171: "The reason for saying that art imitates nature is as follows. Knowledge is the principle of

operation in art. But all of our knowledge is through the senses and taken from sensible, natural things. Hence in artificial things we work to a likeness of natural things. And so imitable natural things are [i.e., are produced] through art, because all nature is ordered to its end by some intellective principle, so that the work of nature thus seems to be the work of intelligence as it proceeds to certain ends through determinate means. And this order is imitated by art in its operation."

147 After much research, scholars conclude that this must refer to the erstwhile (or else extant but now held in camera) Cambridge University dining club, known as the Triangle Club, combining invited-only representatives of the Faculties of Theology, Philosophy and Natural Science. See V. R. S. V. Stiffneck, *Topical References in* Fabula Rustici: *The state of play* (Wisbech: Paratactic Press, 2012), p. 300. See also Donald Wiebe, *Beyond Legitimation: Essays on the Problem of Religious Knowledge* (London: Macmillan, 1994), p. 215, n. 1; *God and the Scientist: Exploring the Work of John Polkinghorne*, eds. Fraser Watts and Christopher C. Knight (London: Routledge, 2012), p. x. Town-lore records that puzzled Cambridge townfolk have for centuries been hard put to decipher the cry, "Will you be triangulating tonight, Harry [or Tom or Dick &c.]?" knurled across the aforementioned King's Parade in the encroaching twilight. See Francis Blomefield, *Collectanea Cantabrigiensa, or Collections relating to Cambridge, University, Town, and County, Containing the Monumental Inscriptions in All the Chapels of the Several Colleges, and Parish Churches in the Town, and in Several Others in the County* (Norwich, 1751).

148 The following MSS do not contain the present scene (lines 3560–3960): [Crozier FR M. a. 172] [Blotting Paper C. P. Mn. I. 17, c. 46r.] [Pink Ties C. P. Mn. I. 18, c. 46r.] [Public Garden C. P. Mc. I. 18. C. 46r.]. See Clydebounde, *The Crozier Manuscript*, pp. 67–88. The comic interruption of rarefied discussion of *Verbum cordis* by burlesque parody of scholastic discussion, immediately before the entry of DEUS, is suggestive of possible influence by the Wakefield Master. See Edminster, *The Preaching Fox*, p. 40. Festive features include comic reversal, profanity, parody, reference to feasting, declamation, invective, insult, hyperbole. See Kolve, *The Play called* Corpus Christi, p. 134 ff., on the comic mockery of the sacred in the cycle-plays.

149 It is to be noted that these characters are feasting on pudding on the Eve of All Souls. Currants and sultanas were lavish delicacies. Perhaps the pudding to which they refer, with its rich ingredients, is a soul [or soul-mass] cake, traditionally referred to as "souls," traditionally given

to "soulers" who went from door to door, often in disguise, crying, "Soul, souls, for a soul-cake; Pray you good mistress, a soul-cake!" (Lucy Etheldred Broadwood and John Alexander Fuller-Maitland, *English County Songs* [London: Leadenhall Press, 1893], pp. 30–31). See Mary Mapes Dodge, ed., *St Nicholas Magazine* (New York: Scribner and Co., 1883), p. 93; Nicholas Rogers, *Hallowe'en: From Pagan Ritual to Party Night* (Oxford: Oxford University Press, 2002), p. 28. See further William Hone, *The Every-day Book and Table Book: Or, Everlasting Calendar of Popular Amusements, Sports, Pastimes, Ceremonies, Manners, Customs, and Events, Incident to Each of the Three Hundred and Sixty-five Days, in Past and Present Times; Forming a Complete History of the Year, Months, and Seasons, and a Perpetual Key to the Almanac; Including Accounts of the Weather, Rules for Health and Conduct, Remarkable and Important Anecdotes, Facts, and Notices, in Chronology, Antiquities, Topography, Biography, Natural History, Art, Science, and General Literature; Derived from the Most Authentic Sources, and Valuable Original Communications, with Poetical Elucidations, for Daily Use and Diversion* (London: T. Tegg, 1830), Vol. 1. See n. 84.

150 The Editor has been unable to trace the significance of these references.

151 The Editor has double-checked these two lines (ll. 3658–60) across the manuscripts where they appear, and notes that she has reckoned them correctly.

152 On the possible connection between the game referred to in this scene and that of the play itself, see Kolve, *The Play called* Corpus Christi, p. 14 ff. Elsewhere in the present play, truth is shown "vnder pretence of play": John Skelton, *Magnyfycence: A Moral Play*, ed. Robert L. Ramsay (London: Routledge, 2018), p. 14. On the unclear boundary between liturgical drama and real events, or the "true tragedy" as supra-real events, transcending verisimilitude, see Tydeman, "An introduction to medieval English theatre," in Beadle, ed., *Cambridge Companion*, p. 5. See also p. 10.

153 This is the first of several cosmic interferences in the play, heralding the arrival of DEUS and the four mystical women at 3960 and 4394 ff., respectively.

154 *Summa Theologiae*, I Q 14 a 3 ad 1; *Summa Contra* Gentiles, IV. 1 (2): "And because in the highest summit of things, God, one finds the most perfect unity – and because everything, the more it is one, is the more powerful and more worthy – it follows that the farther one

gets from the first principle, the greater is the diversity and variation one finds in things. The process of emanation from God must, then, be unified in the principle itself, but multiplied in the lower things which are its terms. In this way, according to the diversity of things, there appears the diversity of the ways, as though these ways began in one principle and terminated in various ends."

155 One notes that the dialogue in this scene takes place between DEUS and Mr No-Nonsense, and not, as one might have expected, between DEUS and Goobet, or DEUS and Thomas. Is this because Goobet has been effectively overthrown, as is the custom for Lords of Misrule? Or is it rather that Goobet and DEUS share an affinity, as indicated at line 84 and lines 4499 ff., or that Goobet, as "simpler," has been edified ahead of the more discursively-confined characters? Even those characters espousing "non-mistical" notions are included in the general dance: presumably even Jacques — for whom *"Realte isn't reale"*—appears to be included in the exaltation; see line 84. See also Edminster, *The Preaching Fox*, p. 37 ff.

156 *Quaestiones Disputatae de Veritate*, Q 1 a 5 resp.

157 *Quaestiones Disputatae de Veritate*, Q 1 a 5 resp. "An astronomer, for example, knowing all the motions of the heavens and the distances between the celestial bodies, would know every eclipse that will occur even for the next hundred years, yet he would not know any one eclipse as a distinct singular so as to have evidential knowledge that it actually exists or not — which a country bumpkin has when he sees an eclipse."

158 *Quaestiones Disputatae de Veritate*, Q 4 a 4 resp. "This difference is also found with respect to the intellectual processions. The word expressed in us by actual consideration and arising, as it were, from a consideration of a thing known previously, or at least from habitual knowledge, does not receive into itself the whole of that from which it had its origin. For, in the conception of one word, the intellect expresses not all but only part of what it possesses in its habitual knowledge. Similarly, what is contained in one conclusion does not express all that was contained virtually in its principle. However, for the divine Word to be perfect, it must express whatever is contained in that from which it had its origin, especially since God sees all things, not in many intuitions, but in one. Consequently, whatever is contained in the Father's knowledge is necessarily and entirely expressed by His only Word and in the very same manner in which all things are contained in His knowledge. In this way it is a true word, whose

intellectual content corresponds to that of its principle. Through His knowledge, moreover, the Father knows Himself, and, by knowing Himself, He knows all other things. Hence, His Word chiefly expresses the Father and, as a result, all other things which the Father knows by knowing Himself. Therefore, because the Son is a word that perfectly expresses the Father, the Son expresses all creatures. This sequence is outlined by the words of Anselm, who said that by uttering Himself the Father uttered all creatures." One hazards that this play exalts the sense of sight of its audience members in construing mundane seeing as an advance sight of the Beatific vision, and dramatizes their own incorporation into salvation history, as well perhaps as advising them of the dangers or pointlessness of what may appear to be trivial preoccupations, such as scholastic discussions of truth, or variously propositional or nihilistic conclusions of the same. Perhaps, following Aristotle, the sense of sight was regarded as a subcategory of the sense of touch. See Kolve, *The Play called* Corpus Christi, chapter five.

159 Aristotle, *De Anima*, 2, ix, 422b 17-424a15; Aquinas, *In De Anima*, *lectiones* 22-23.

160 Psalm 38.4.

161 Dante Alighieri, *Purgatorio*, 31.104. [Manuscript irregularities; early fragments of the play, such as [MSS Crozier FR M. a. 172] [Crozier II D. a l. 1554] [Blotting Paper C. P. Mn. I. 17 c. 46r.] [Pink Ties C. P. Mn. I. 18 c. 46r.] and [Unbound Fragments C. P. Mn. I. 19, c. 46r.] omit the verses of the four women]. See Ezra Clydebounde, *Manuscript Inconsistences of the* Fabula Rustici (Cambridge: RO Press, 1981), p. 47. Scholars debate the choice and significance of these female figures by the playwright[s]. The four figures are silent in the history of theology except insofar as they are represented indirectly (or directly, in the case of Diotima, though at two removes) by men, and did not commit their ideas to written form, in some cases this being thematised. They are also known for their inspiration and salvation of specific men [Socrates, Gregory of Nyssa, Augustine and Dante, respectively]. See further Preface, p. xx. Does their circular dance mimic the circling of the transcendentals at lines 1565 ff.? And is it comically anticipated by Act Three, Scene Two, which precedes the entry of DEUS? The mention of swooning may also be significant. See Barry Windeatt, "The Art of Swooning in Middle English," in *Medieval Latin and Middle English Literature*, eds. Christopher Cannon and Maura Nolan (Cambridge: Boydell & Brewer, 2013), pp. 211-30.

162 162 MSS [Crozier FR M. a. 172] [Crozier II D. a l. 1554] [Blotting Paper C. P. Mn. I. 17 c. 46r.] [Pink Ties C. P. Mn. I. 18 c. 46r.] and [Unbound Fragments C. P. Mn. I. 19, c. 46r.] omit lines 1347–1426. See further, Clydebounde, *The Crozier Manuscript*, pp. 56-80.

163 Plato, *Symposium*, 201d-204c.

164 Barry Windeatt, "The Discourse of Sighs in Medieval English Literature," *Chaucer Review*, 58 (2023), pp. 442-55.

165 Gregory, Bishop of Nyssa, *The Life of Saint Macrina*, ed. and trans. Kevin Corrigan (Eugene, Oregon: Wipf and Stock Publishers, 2001), p. 36.

166 For the metaphysical significance of such a posture, see Peter the Chanter, *The Christian at Prayer: An Illustrated Prayer Manual*, ed. Richard C. Trexler (New York: Medieval and Early Renaissance Studies, 1987), e.g. Mode 2 fig. 1 and 2.

167 *The Life of Saint Macrina*, p. 48.

168 Saint Augustine, *Confessiones* 6.2.2.

169 See Barry Windeatt, "Chaucer's Tears," *Critical Survey*, 30 (2018) 69-88. On lamentation, commiseration and compassion in mediaeval drama, and possible parallels with the "Planctus Mariae" trope, see Sandro Sticca, *The Planctus Mariae in the Dramatic Tradition of the Middle Ages*, trans. Joseph R. Berrigan (Athens and London: University of Georgia Press, 1988). On Monica's salvific yet irritating weeping, see Augustine, *Confessiones* 3.11, 3.12. See also Margaret R. Miles, *Desire and Delight: A New Reading of Augustine's* Confessions (Eugene, Oregon: Wipf and Stock, 1991), pp. 81-82. Monica's weeping is said to have annoyed both SS. Ambrose and Augustine.

170 See further, Tatyana Ferdwalde, *Theological intimations in the manuscripts of the* Fabula Rustici (Oxford: Hypotactic Press, 1961), p. 30.

171 Reference to the "scaffolde" confirms Robinson's analysis of stagecraft from this period. See Robinson, *Studies*, pp. 23 f.; also Meredith and Tailby, *The Staging*, p. 74; see Miyajima, *The Theatre of Man: Dramatic Technique and Stagecraft in the English Mediaeval Moral Plays*, p. 45.

172 [Turn] [Goobet] [Floorboard MS C. P. I. 21, c. 46r.] only. The four dancing women may invoke the intercession of the four daughters of God, as at Psalm 85 line 10, comically anticipated by the four drunken tribesmen wearing animal tails. On Beatrice as co-redemptrix, compare Sticca, *The Planctus Mariae*, chapter two. On artificial animal parts, see Meredith and Tailby, *The Staging*, pp. 117-22.

173 See Catherine of Siena, *The Dialogue*, trans. Suzanne Noffke, OP (Mahwah, NJ: Paulist Press, 1981), pp. 161–78.

174 A reference to Geoffrey Chaucer's translation of Boethius' *Consolation of Philosophy*: "that the firmament stont derked by wete ploungy cloudes" (lines 154–55): Richard Morris, ed. (Project Gutenberg EBook, 2013), #42083.

175 It is not known where the playwright(s) envisage(s) Beatrice's finishing point on the stage or above it, since she is already positioned on the "scaffolde." See n. 145 and n. 171. It was common for the scaffold to indicate prideful or avaricious characters, as in *The Castle of Perseverance*. But in the present play, it is indicative of purity and exaltation. It is not specified whether Jacques has by this point descended from the scaffold, or remains aloft (see line 3534). One assumes from the pointing, "*All the characters join the dance*" (line 4499), that he has descended and joined the dancing pageant. His encouraging interjection, "*Ah oui!*" (line 3534), is suggestive of *afflatus*, or exalted alignment with the mysteries.

176 An example of dramatic understatement. Ed.

177 [Where is restored all manner of thing | Both meat dishes and salted codfish and brimming clusters of bullace plums]

178 [The Tree of Knowledge | Is for our Salvation]

179 [In knowing, all things are bound together]

180 There is speculation concerning the implied salvific synaesthesia in line 4527–28 which is said to "vnbotton | Oure kyndes' Falle." See further, Clydebounde, *The Crozier Manuscript*, p. 872; *Saturated Sensorium: Principles of Perception & Mediation in the Middle Ages*, ed. Hans Henrik Lohfert Jorgensen, Henning Laugerud, and Laura Katrine Skinnebach (Aarhus: Aarhus University Press, 2014), pp. 174–79. See also Barry Windeatt, "Towards a Gestural Lexicon of Medieval English Romance," in E. Archibald, M. G. Leitch and C. Saunders, eds., *Romance Rewritten: The Evolution of Middle English Romance. A Tribute to Helen Cooper* (Cambridge: Boydell & Brewer, 2018 [Studies in Medieval Romance]), pp. 133–52.

181 [Our bodily senses | help to undo the Fall]

182 [The truth of God, and being, and Beauty, shall be tied together]

183 [And a perfect accord between God and man | which truth shall never divide] or [From which Truth shall never be divided]

184 [Man's soul in bliss shall now be edified]

185 [Pepper, the seed of the peony, sweet liquorice]. Evidence of textual interference, corruption or interpolation. See *Ludus Coventriae*, ed. James Orchard Halliwell (London: The Shakespeare Society, 1841), p. 22. On the idyllic conflation of the verdant East Anglian landscape and Paradise in these alliterative lines, see Philippa Maddern, "Imagining the Unchanging Land: East Anglians represent their landscape, 1350–1500," in *Medieval East Anglia*, ed. Christopher Harper-Bill (Woodbridge: The Boydell Press, 2005), pp. 52–67, p. 66. See also Wattle-Sprye, *Textual Interferences*.

186 A further reference to the circular dance of transcendentals, and of persons, human and divine, one speculates. Ed.

BIBLIOGRAPHY

Primary sources cited in the play or otherwise suggested are indicated below, followed by secondary sources. Works marked with an asterisk [*] may prove difficult to locate, perhaps owing to small print-runs or lack of open access compliance.

ANCIENT PHILOSOPHY
Plato, *Symposium* (385–370 BC)
Aristotle, *De Anima* (c. 350 BC)
— , *Metaphysics* (c. 350 BC)
Liber De Causis (c. 850)

DRAMATIC WORKS
Ludus Coventriae (c.1450–1500)
The Barbers Playe of the *Chester Mystery Cycle* (early fourteenth century)
The Castle of Perseverance (1400–1425)
Wakefield Mystery Plays. Mactacio Abel
Skelton, John. *Magnyfycence: A Moral Play* (1516)

THEOLOGICAL WORKS
Saint Augustine. *Soliloquies* (386–87)
— , *Confessiones* (c. 397–400)
— , *De Doctrina Christiana* (396/7–426/7)
— , *De Libero Arbitrio* (388–95)
— , *De Trinitate* (318–419 or 426)
Gregory, Bishop of Nyssa. *The Life of Saint Macrina* (written between c. 380 and 383)
Peter the Chanter (d. 1179). *The Christian at Prayer: An Illustrated Prayer Manual*
Saint Thomas Aquinas. *De Ente et Essentia* (c. 1252–56)
— , *Summa Theologiae* (1266–73)
— , *Quaestiones Disputatae de Veritate* (1256–59)
— , *De Potentia* (1265–66)
— , *Commentary on Aristotle's* Physics (1266–72)
— , *Summa Contra Gentiles* (1259–65)
— , *Quaestiones Disputatae de Anima*
Catherine of Siena. *The Dialogue of Divine Providence* (1377–78)

POETICAL WORKS
Chaucer, Geoffrey. *Boece* (c. 1380)

— , *The House of Fame* (c. 1374-85)

Dante Alighieri. *Purgatorio* (c. 1313-14)

Cavendish, Margaret. The Right Honourable, the Lady Margaret Countess of Newcastle. "Of Many Worlds in This World" and *Nature calls a
Councell, which was Motion, Figure, matter,* and *Life,* to advise about
making the World. *Poems, and Fancies Written.* London: T. R. for J.
Martin, and J. Allestrye at the Bell in Saint Pauls Church Yard, 1653.

CAMBRIDGE PLATONIST WORKS OF THEOLOGY AND PHILOSOPHY

Greville, Robert. *The Nature of Christ* [1640] facsimile. London: Gregg
International. 1969.

Conway, Anne. (Viscountess Conway). *The Principles of the Most Ancient
and Modern Philosophy.* Cambridge: Cambridge University Press. 1996.
(written between 1631 and 1679)

SECONDARY SOURCES

Agamben, Giorgio. 2005. *State of Exception.* Translated by Kevin Attell.
Chicago: Chicago University Press.

Ayer, A. J. 1935. "The Criterion of Truth." *Analysis* 3: 28-32.

Bakhtin, Mikhail. 1984. *Rabelais and his World.* Translated by Helene
Iswolsky. Bloomington, IN: Indiana University Press.

— , 1981. *The Dialogic Imagination.* Translated by Caryl Emerson and
Michael Holquist. Austin, TX: University of Texas Press.

Barber, C. L. 1959. *Shakespeare's Festive Comedy.* Princeton, NJ: Princeton
University Press.

Beadle, H. R. L. 1977. "The Medieval Drama of East Anglia: Studies in
Dialect, Documentary Records and Stagecraft." Ph.D. Thesis, University
of York (uk.bl.ethos.449288).

Beadle, Richard, ed. 1994. *The Cambridge Companion to Medieval English
Theatre.* Cambridge: Cambridge University Press.

Bernanos, Georges. 1937/1965. *The Diary of a Country Priest.* Translated by
Pamela Morris. New York: Carroll and Graf Publishers.

Blanchette, Oliva. 1992. *The Perfection of the Universe According to Aquinas: A teleological cosmology.* Pennsylvania: the Pennsylvania State
University Press.

Blomefield, Francis. 1751. *Collectanea Cantabrigiensa, or Collections relating
to Cambridge, University, Town, and County, Containing the Monumental
Inscriptions in All the Chapels of the Several Colleges, and Parish Churches
in the Town, and in Several Others in the County.* Norwich.

Breton, Stanislas. 1962. "La deduction Thomiste des catégories." *Revue
Philosophique de Louvain,* third Series 60. 65 (1962): 5-32.

Broadwood, Lucy Etheldred and Fuller-Maitland, John Alexander. 1983. *English County Songs*. London: Leadenhall Press.

Bruyne, E. de. 1946. *Études d'esthétique médiévale*. Louvain: Éditions de l'Institut Supérieur de Philosophie.

Clark, Stephen R. L. 1977. *The Moral Status of Animals*. Oxford: Oxford University Press.

Coldewey, John C. 2008."The non-cycle plays and the East Anglian tradition." In Beadle, ed. *Cambridge Companion to Medieval English Theatre*, 189-210. Cambridge: Cambridge University Press.

Cornford, F. M. 1908. *Microcosmographia Academica: Being a Guide for the Young Academic Politician*. Cambridge: Bowes & Bowes.

*Clydebounde, Ezra. 1980. *The Crozier Manuscript*. Oxford: Old Headington Press.

* —, 1981. *Manuscript Inconsistences of the* Fabula Rustici. Cambridge: RO Press.

Davidson, Donald. 1990. "The Structure and Content of Truth." *The Journal of Philosophy* 87. 6: 279-326.

Dickinson, J.C. 1961. *Monastic Life in Medieval England*. London: A. & C. Black.

Diller, Hans-Jurgen. 2002. "Laughter in Medieval English Drama: A Critique of Modernizing and Historical Analyses." *Comparative Drama* 36: 1-19.

*Dilly-Dilly, Ronald. 1998. "A Response to Mayheme: Solemn Prolepsis in Low-Life Scenes." *Elliptika* 2: 677-712.

Dodge, Mary Mapes, ed. 1883. *St Nicholas Magazine*. New York: Scribner and Co.

Eco, Umberto. 1988. *The Aesthetics of Thomas Aquinas*. Translated by Hugh Bredin. London: Radius.

Edminster, Warren. 2005. *The Preaching Fox: Festive Subversion in the Plays of the Wakefield Master*. London: Routledge.

*Ferdwalde, Tatyana. 1961. *Theological footnotes to the manuscript of the* Fabula Rustici. Oxford: Hypotactic Press.

*Fitchmeyer, Tatyana. 1981. *Gott oder Bumpkin: Was soll es sein?* Munich: kühle Bergpresse.

Frege, Gottlob. 1960. "On Concept and Object [1892]." In *Translations from the Philosophical Writings of Gottlob Frege*, 42-55. Edited by Peter Geach and Max Black. Oxford: Basil Blackwell.

— , 1956. "The thought: A Logical Inquiry." *Mind* 65. 259 (July): 289-311.

*Freluquet, Marie de. 2000. *Que toute chair mortelle se taise: Devenir animal face à l'univocité de l'être*. Tours: Presse Winston.

Granger, Penny. 2009. *The N-Town Play: Drama and Liturgy in Medieval East Anglia*. Cambridge: D. S. Brewer.

Harris, John Wesley. 1992. *Medieval theatre in Context*. New York: Routledge.

Hoenicke Moore, Michael E. 2003. "Demons and the Battle for Souls at Cluny." *Sciences Religieuses* 32.4: 485-97.

Hone, William. 1893. *The Every-day book and Table Book or Everlasting Calendar of Popular Amusements, Sports, Pastimes, Ceremonies, Manners, Customs, and Events, incident to Each of the three Hundred and Sixty-five Days, in past and present times; forming a complete history of the year, months, and seasons, and a perpetual key to the almanac.* London: Thomas Tegg and Son. Volume Two.

James, John. 1967. . . . *mmm* . . . *ah yes.* London: Ferry Press.

Kolve, V. A. 1996. *The Play called* Corpus Christi. Stanford, CA: Stanford University Press.

Lepow, Lauren. 1990. *Enacting the Sacrament.* Rutherford: Fairleigh Dickinson University Press.

Lerud, Theodore K. 2008. *Memory, Images and the English* Corpus Christi *Drama.* New York: Palgrave Macmillan.

Libera, Alain de. 2007. *Archéologie du Sujet 1: Naissance du Sujet.* Paris: J. Vrin.

Lohfert Jørgensen, Hans Henrik, Laugerud, Henning, and Skinnebach, Laura Katrine, eds. 2015. *The Saturated Sensorium: Principles of Perception and Mediation in the Middle Ages.* Aarhus: Aarhus University Press.

Maddern, Philippa. 2005. "Imagining the Unchanging Land: East Anglians represent their landscape, 1350-1500." In *Medieval East Anglia*, 52-67. Edited by Christopher Harper-Bill. Woodbridge: The Boydell Press.

Mayaud, Pierre-Noël, ed. 1991. *Le Problème de L'Individuation.* Paris: J. Vrin.

*Mayheme, Eric. 1978. *Prophetic Invocations in the Impyngton Playe.* Volume 1. Mayfair, London: Uppity Press.

McGrath, Matthew. 2000. *Between Deflationism and Correspondence.* New York: Garland Publishing.

McIntosh, Angus, Samuels, M. L. and Benskin, Michael, eds. 1986. *A Linguistic Atlas of Late Medieval English.* 4 volumes. Aberdeen: Aberdeen University Press.

Meredith, Peter and Tailby, John E. eds. 1983. *The Staging of Religious Drama in Europe in the later Middle Ages: Texts and Documents in English translation.* Kalamazoo: Medieval Institute Publications.

Milbank, John. 2015. "Manifestation and Procedure: Trinitarian Metaphysics after Albert the Great and Thomas Aquinas." *Tomismo Creativo: letture Contemporanee del Doctor Communis*, 41-117. Edited by Marco Salvioli, OP. Bologna: E S D.

— , and Pickstock, C. J. C. 2000. *Truth in Aquinas.* London: Routledge.

Miles, Margaret R. 1991. *Desire and Delight: A New Reading of Augustine's Confessions.* Eugene, OR: Wipf and Stock.

Millet Salter, Frederick, and Wilson Greg, Walter. 1936. *The Trial & Flagellation with Other Studies in the* Chester Cycle. Oxford: Oxford University Press, for the Malone Society.

Mitchell, W. J. T. 1986. *Iconology: Image, Text, Ideology*. Chicago: Chicago University Press.

Miyajima, Sumiko. 1977. *Theatre of Man: Dramatic Technique and Stage-craft in the English Mediaeval Moral Plays*. Clevedon: Clevedon Printing Co., Ltd.

*Mooncalf, Matilda. 2001. "Goobet's kenosis: *Fabula Rustici* as a Biblical play after all?" *Études en matière médiévale* 23.6: 871-99.

Muir, Lynette. 1995. *The Biblical Drama of Medieval Europe*. Cambridge: Cambridge University Press.

Narcisse OP, Gilbert. 1997. *Les Raisons de Dieu: Arguments de convenance et Esthétique théologie selon St Thomas d'Aquin et Hans Urs von Balthasar*. Fribourg: Editions Universitaires Fribourg Suisse.

Nelson, Alan H., ed. 1989. *Records of Early English Drama: Cambridge*. 2 volumes. Toronto: Toronto University Press.

O'Rourke, Fran. 1992. *Pseudo-Dionysius and the Metaphysics of Aquinas*. Leiden: E. J. Brill.

Pickstock, Catherine. 2001. *Thomas d'Aquin et la quête eucharistique*. Paris: Editions Ad Solem.

*Plankton, Miriam. 1971. "The Staging of the Impyngton Play(s)." *The Ohio Journal of Medieval Theatre* 29.1 (March): 402-99.

Priest, Graham. 1995. *Beyond the Limits of Thought*. Cambridge: Cambridge University Press.

Pilhuj, Katja. 2019. *Women and Geography on the Early Modern English Stage* (Gendering the Late Medieval and Early Modern World). Amsterdam: Amsterdam University Press.

Pouillon, Henri. 1946. "La Beauté, Propriété *transcendentale* chez les Scolastiques, 1220-1270." *Archives d'Histoire Doctrinale et Littéraire du Moyen Age* 15: 263-328.

Prosser, Eleanor. 1961. *Drama and Religion in the English Mystery Plays: a re-evaluation*. Stanford, CA: Stanford University Press.

Quine, W. V. O. 1970. *Philosophy of Logic*. Englewood Cliffs, NJ: Prentice Hall.

Ramsey, F. P. 1927. "Facts and Propositions." *Proceedings of the Aristotelian Society*, Supplementary Volume 7: 153-70.

Robinson, J. W. 1991. *Studies in Fifteenth-Century Stagecraft*. Kalamazoo, MI: Western Michigan University.

Rogers, Nicholas. 2002. *Halloween: From Pagan Ritual to Party Night*. Oxford: Oxford University Press.

Schell, Edgar. 1983. *Strangers and Pilgrims: From* The Castle of Perseverance *to* King Lear. Chicago: Chicago University Press.

Scherb, Victor I. 2001. *Staging Faith: East Anglian Drama in the Later Middle Ages.* London: Associated University Presses.

Sandro, Sticca. 1988. *The* Planctus Mariae *in the Dramatic Tradition of the Middle Ages.* Translated by Joseph R. Berrigan. Athens and London: University of Georgia Press.

*Stiffneck, V. R. S. V. 2012. *Topical References in* Fabula Rustici: *The state of play.* Wisbech: Paratactic Press.

Tatarkiewicz, Wladyslaw. 1970. *History of Aesthetics.* Vol. 1. The Hague: De Gruyter Mouton.

*Tremblay, Moses. 2012. "Qui est Monsieur No-Nonsense? Au cœur de *Fabula Rustici.*" *Etudes de théâtre médiéval obscure* 4. 3: 344–402.

Twycross, Meg. 2008. "The theatricality of medieval English plays." In Beadle and Fletcher, eds., *Cambridge Companion to Medieval English Theatre,* 37–84. Cambridge: Cambridge University Press.

Tydeman, William. 2008. "An introduction to medieval English theatre." In Beadle and Fletcher, eds., *The Cambridge Companion to Medieval English theatre,* 1–36. Cambridge: Cambridge University Press.

Velde, Rudi te. 1995. *Participation and Substantiality in Thomas Aquinas.* London: E. J. Brill.

*Wattle-Sprye, Maurice. 1970. *Textual Interferences in* Fabula Rustici. Blenheim Bridge, Oxon: Flotsam and Spindrift Press.

Watts, Fraser, and Knight, Christopher C., eds. 2012. *God and the Scientist: Exploring the Work of John Polkinghorne.* London: Routledge.

Wiebe, Donald. 1994. *Beyond Legitimation: Essays on the Problem of Religious Knowledge.* London: Macmillan.

Windeatt, B. A. C. 2023. "The Discourse of Sighs in Medieval English Literature." *Chaucer Review* 58: 442–55.

— , 2021. "The Body Language of Malory's *Le Morte Darthur.*" In *Medieval Romance, Arthurian Literature: Essays in Honour of Elizabeth Archibald,* 143–57. Edited by A. S. G. Edwards. Cambridge: D. S. Brewer.

— , 2018. "Chaucer's Tears." *Critical Survey* 30: 69–88.

— , 2013. "The Art of Swooning in Middle English." In *Medieval Latin and Middle English Literature,* edited by Christopher Cannon and Maura Nolan, 211–30. Suffolk: Boydell & Brewer.

— , 2012. "La3amon's Gestures: Body Language in the Brut." In *Reading La3amon's Brut: Approaches and Explorations,* edited by R. Allen, J. Roberts and C. Weinberg, 253–67. Amsterdam: Rodopi.

Wycliffe, John. 1869. "A Sermon against Miracle Plays." In Mätzner, Eduard, ed., *Altenglische Sprachproben,* I, Part II, 222–42. Berlin.

INDEX

www.ingramcontent.com/pod-product-compliance
Lightning Source LLC
Chambersburg PA
CBHW021141090426
42740CB00008B/888